Helping Hands

Many days I wake up still thinking it is all just a nightmare, for there is no way that within 10 months my life could really be turned upside down to this extent. How is this even possible I ask myself? And then I would keep working on this book to focus on the "unbelievable" and "amazing" gifts of time and support that those around us provided. Creative and generous assistance from family, friends, acquaintances, and total strangers. Without this kindness, I know we would never have survived physically or financially. In the past, I would say to others who were going through a difficult time, "If you need anything let me know." It is unbelievable how much your daily life is impacted by traumas and tragedies. And it is unbelievable how gracious and kind people are who come to your aid. I hope this book gives you additional creative ideas on how to help others or gives you the freedom to ask for help when you are in need of assistance.

"As I worked with Sheilla on the publishing of this book, I was struck by the amazing generosity and creativity of the people that helped Sheilla and her husband. This book captures it perfectly, providing ideas that I can use when trying to help someone in my life."

Julie Norris, Graphics and Publishing Coach

"It brightened my day when a hospital kit arrived from Sheilla the day before my husband went into surgery. It contained healthy snacks, a note pad, pens, and other items with an easy-carry, lightweight bag."

Sharron Cadieux, Editor

Design and Layout: Julie Norris
Editor: Sharron Cadieux
Collaboration Team: Scott Baughman, Dana Bishop, Ruth Casto, Patty Green, Judi Jagger, Colleen Miller, Claudia Sadler-Gerhardt, PhD, and Cathy Schindler.

Collaborative Results 778 McCauley Rd.
Suite #120 Stow OH 44224

Ordering Guidelines: Special discounts are available on quantity purchases. Place orders using the address above or the website, www.cresults.info.

Helping Hands

A Guide to Helping Others Through Trauma and Tragedy

Written By
Sheilla Reydak

A compilation of remarkable stories about the amazing kindness of family, friends, and strangers that lifted us up following an inconceivable series of devastating life events.

Dedication

Without the amazing encouragement of my family and friends, this book would not exist. They are both the source of the content as they gave us the strength to make it through multiple crises followed by ongoing therapy and challenges. Without their involvement, I would not have thought to share our story nor stayed on track to its completion. I would have been consumed by the incredible amount of work it takes to be injured and to move forward.

I want to thank my husband, my sister, my graphics coach, my collaboration team, and the group of women I call my inspiration team.

I can never say enough to thank everyone who helped us over the last four years. I could not have survived let alone written this book without you.

Contents

Inspiration

Inspiration

I wrote this book to inspire individuals to be creative as they help others through a trauma or tragedy. I was always the go-to person to help people through a financial or work-related struggle. I dug in and knew exactly what to do in order to be helpful. However, when it came to people who were struggling with a family challenge or a medical challenge my standard line was, "Let me know if you need anything." And, though I really meant this with all my heart, I rarely ever heard from anyone.

Through our recent events, I realized that when I helped people through a financial or work-related struggle that I took a more focused approach. I would say something such as, "I would be happy to help you with your resume, cover letter, and set up your office space. I have time next Tuesday or Wednesday if you would like to get together." Using this approach, people knew what I would be interested in doing to help and, therefore, felt comfortable asking for assistance.

So, while I was lying in bed trying to recover from almost being killed when a car crashed into our post office, I started this book. A book inspired by friends from church after I would tell them how amazed I was at what an injured person needs and how grateful I was that there were people sharing their time and talents to help me with those needs. I never would have had the energy to fight my way back without all of the help and love that I received.

I realized that the help I sought was the help offered by those individuals who approached me the way I coached people with a work issue. The people who said, "I clean for my daughter and would be very happy to come over on Thursday mornings to spend an hour or two cleaning for you. I find cleaning to be a stress relief for me." Wow. This gave me all the information I needed. I knew what this person liked to do. I knew when it would be a good time for her to do it. And, I knew that she wanted to do it for me.

Plus, though an injured or sick person may seem to be on top of things, the medication and total focus on healing can make it difficult to make a lot of decisions. And there are already so many medical and logistical decisions to be made that having some guidance on options to make one's life just a little bit easier are, in my world, greatly appreciated. The ideas in this book were of great help to me. Understand that others may be experiencing different circumstances or have a different approach to their recovery. That is why the premise is to offer and then leave it in their hands.

This book was inspired to be about helping others understand what it took me being injured to learn. First, that even though people may have had their life the way they wanted it before they were injured does not mean that everything they had in place will work for them as they recover or strive to live a new restricted life. Second, there are so many wonderful things that can help an injured person based on your talents and time. The focus of this book is to share the numerous ways one can help others faced with all types of challenges. Ideas which will then inspire even more ideas.

As a result, I was not planning to share my particular trauma. The book was not about me. It was about helping others. So, my first rendition of the book included the following paragraph which basically outlines what happened:

My husband had a hip replacement. While he was recovering, I was almost killed by a car. While I was still learning to walk again, 30 feet of our 35 foot basement wall collapsed and everything in the basement was destroyed. After being evacuated for a month, the day we moved back into a yet unfinished but livable house, my husband had a stroke.

The first readers of the book encouraged me to write more. They told me that, even if it is difficult to write, readers want to know more about what happened. If you would like to learn more of our own story, please visit the "Journal" section at the end of this book.

I really am not sure how we are pulling this off at this time except that we have been blessed with an incredible support group comprised of people who we know and angels who we barely knew or never knew in the past. Their smiles and positive energy are what have kept us moving forward as we work to create a different life for ourselves.

The amazing result was that people who we knew and people who we had never met rallied to help with my care and my husband's care. It is this that is the inspiration of this book.

Philosophy

Reinventing Your World

Thank you for taking the time to understand that any one of the events we have faced continue to be very stressful. Healing is hugely mental. A person needs encouragement, guidance, and support from others. Or at least that is what I needed. I needed the stories where people were told they would not be able to walk and they proved it was possible. Those stories got me through. At some point we may need to accept that we will no longer be able to do what we once could do and we must therefore create new interests within our capabilities. I personally feel it is too early to accept this right after a new trauma. Initially, when someone would tell me to accept, I needed to remember the stories of people who defied the averages. This helped me focus on improving every day and keep believing that I could regain enough functionality to remain independent. There is no other way for it to happen. You need those around you to help without enabling. Without the knowledge of our friends and professional colleagues, I fear what our outcome would have been.

I met with a business associate yesterday who complemented me on moving forward with work at this time. Financially, I of course have no choice, though having no choice also keeps me grounded. She told me how during her psychology class, her professor said to recognize that if a person went through three traumatic events, they could easily be at the brink. This made sense to me based on the research I have used in my work regarding how the amygdala within the brain needs time to recover, before another similar event. If it does not have time to recover, the brain's reaction is then more severe to an event and requires more time to recover.

You, through your actions, can be the source that helps people to keep moving and keep positive. Your actions of helping show them they are loved and give them strength to continue the fight. This is to be done while ensuring you are living your own life, for as we have proven, life can take a terrible turn at any point. Share of yourself when you are able as a part of living your life to the fullest.

Gifts Given Promote Healing

The blessing of so many people coming to my rescue has given me the strength to push through this ordeal. I am still in the midst of it all right now so I don't know how it will all end—no one knows how it will be from moment to moment, especially when we face life-long issues.

I know that, prior to this event, caring for friends who were injured or sick was not one of my natural gifts. With family, I just jumped in assuming they needed me. For friends, if there was a job loss, an emotional crisis, a financial concern, or a career challenge—I was your go-to person. I would rally around these types of traumas giving it my all in order to help move a person past the devastating stress. However, when a friend was sick or hurt, I tried to be supportive by saying, "Let me know if you need anything." I just was not comfortable putting my nose into their business on such a personal matter. When I was a child, my parents were very independent, private people who never asked for help.

So, though it is not always easy to discern how to approach a situation, it is my belief that any approach from the heart shows you care. And once we accept the challenge that different people see support from varying perspectives, we can move forward by offering, listening, gently questioning, and respecting without offense.

Now, having years of loving care by so many under my belt, I have discovered some unique alternatives for sharing concern—ideas that straddle the delicate balance of offering from our natural God-given strengths. Speaking from personal experience, some of us are just not equipped to offer a meal but do have other skills which can be of assistance.

The most important thing to remember is that there is no gesture too small. Your gift for one person may be a single note. For another person it may include visits with full care. We are not asked to be all things to all people. Allow yourself to be guided and never judge your own or anyone else's contribution. Remember we never know the scars and experiences of those around us. Not everyone can handle hospitals, illness, or pain.

Some have experienced serious trauma related to an event or situation which they may or may not choose to share. Give where your gifts guide you. Accept, that when in need, others might not behave as we would in the situation—this does not mean that they do not care about us.

❧ No Gift Too Small

I start by sharing my most important opinion—there is never a gift or action too small when from the heart. It is too easy to feel as if we need to make some type of grand gesture which then paralyzes us from moving forward either because we can't think of what to do or never find the chunk of time to do it.

My husband has always been the most amazing person in this way. Out of nowhere, we will be dining on our favorite ice cream and he will buy an extra container to drop at a sick or stressed-out friend's home. The fact that we have not called ahead, the concept of knowing what flavor they like, or the concern that they may not even like ice cream never enters his mind—all these questions would totally stop me in my tracks. If the person then asks for us to come in, sometimes we can and sometimes we are not able. If we are not invited inside, we are not offended.

Throughout this book I will share stories and examples of things that people have done for me or told me about. Some things are relationship-oriented supporting the person in their thinking and emotional well being. Other items are very tactical and task-oriented, supporting our need to get things done during a time when it is not possible or overwhelming. People need emotional as well as daily task support.

We all think of food when someone is injured, sick, or grieving. The gift of food is an amazing, critical gift during a tough time. I can't imagine where we would have been throughout my recovery without the constant gift of meals and snacks. I wish I had the fabulous cooking talent of others—so, how do the rest of us offer help? Throughout this, I have learned so many additional wonderful ideas that would better match my talents.

So whether you choose to read this entire work, flip to a specific heading that matches your talents, or randomly select a page to complete, the journey is one of loving involvement.

The Church Involvement

In my case, our Sunday school class provided emotional and daily task support—an abundance of food, emotional support, and so much more. Women from my church inspired me to write this book. Food arrived daily as I continued to be confined to bed and my husband recovered from his hip surgery. The group followed the doctor's instructions that I eat a high protein diet. Close friends as well as people whom we had only greeted on Sundays came and visited when they brought the food. Many were able to stay and join us for dinner.

A decision can be made within a church as to whether this is a mission that they would like to provide, not only for church members in need but also for others in the community who might face a tragedy. Unfortunately, as much as one church would like to support an entire community of people in need, we know that this is not possible. Therefore, just like our church at one time joined forces with other churches to build a local Habitat for Humanity house, this could be a project where churches or organizations gather together to form a Christian Community Foundation. It would be wonderful to be able help anyone going through a challenging life experience including health issues, injuries, lost employment, home crises, family loss, or emotional distress.

Life is Not Normal

I loved our home! We were in the process of updating, doing much of the work ourselves. I never realized how much being injured could change the organization and function of a home. The medical equipment, additional paperwork, and medical supplies took over our home. Since we were not able to run normal errands, we needed to stock up on frequently used items—where does it all get stored? Is there furniture that needs to be moved for a wheelchair or walker?

Reality is different now. Is the person more comfortable in bed, on the couch, or in a recliner? Do they need big supportive pillows, a bed tray, a basket to hold necessities within reach, or a different type of technology such as a wireless laptop or tablet? Does the person need duplicate items on different floors? Perhaps you could provide transportation? Are they able to lift items, change light bulbs, or access items found on the floor?

If you are inspired to help someone through a difficult time but just not sure what to do, explore some of the ideas within this book or use this to inspire something completely new as I have been so inspired by all the wonderful things friends, family, and strangers did for my husband and me.

The Impossible Plan

When my husband had his hip replacement surgery, we had a lot of preparation time to plan so I thought I was fully on top of things. The challenge is that the doctors never tell you everything you might need so there tend to be medical supplies or life supplies that require extra trips to the pharmacy or to other non-typical stores. Also, when people are not feeling well they may want items to eat that are not their normal food choice—the traditional comfort food items such as chicken noodle soup. Sometimes regular food just does not taste right so it may be important to buy a nutritional supplement like a protein drink.

All of these errands, when one is living on little sleep and concerned about leaving a person alone, can be draining. I know I would go to the store as quickly as possible, afraid that my husband would need my assistance while I was gone. I would quickly try to find items that would work for him. Then I would find out that some items would not work and I would have extra items sitting around that I was afraid to return because I could not leave my husband alone.

In summary, even when a person has time to plan for a surgery or other event, the person and the caretaker really appreciate the help offered by friends and family.

Guide

Routine Activities

Sometimes I repeat myself because the thought is just so important to me. This one bears repeating. I always used to say, "Let me know if you need anything." Though sincere, very few people ever called. Why? Because it does not seem kind to ask someone to do something they would hate doing or be unable to do. And unless you know someone really well, you don't know what they might enjoy doing.

As the injured person, I already was dependent on people to do almost everything for me. I greatly appreciated all of the help being offered from friends and even strangers. Just trying to get better was actually exhausting. Trying to navigate the medical world was like trying to learn a new career.

I really did need help and thankfully so many people encouraged me to accept the help being offered. My first hospital visitors brought me a pad and pen, and told me to list what I needed so that friends could provide solutions.

Even with all that encouragement, I did not want to put anyone in the position of having to tell me that I was asking for something that was not possible. I did not want to ask a person who might have allergies to cleaning chemicals to clean my bathroom. Or, someone who might have outside allergies to mow my lawn. How was I to know who to ask for what? What if the person has back issues and I ask them to move furniture for me?

When everyone is being so kind to you, you want to be considerate of their interests and abilities when asking for help. It is natural to be concerned about the time they are taking out of their day. A common saying is, "If you want something done, ask a busy person." The challenge is that when you need so much help, you never want to feel as if you are being a burden.

So, here is a possible approach. When you offer to help someone who is struggling from an illness, tragedy, trauma, or sometimes simply a difficult time; provide an offer with extra information about how you might like to help. Provide information about what types of things you enjoy doing. Provide guidelines on what time you have available. Explain if you have a physical limitation.

Some examples would be:

- Do you need any help cleaning? I am a fastidious cleaning machine. I clean for my daughter once a week and have Wednesday mornings for two hours that I could come over and do some cleaning for you.

- Do you need help with your flower beds or yard work? I love being outside on nice days and could swing by a few times over the summer if you give me guidelines of what I should and should not touch. I could call you and let you know when I will be there but it would be best if I could pop over when I have an hour or two.

Throughout this book you will find ideas that people suggested and that were of incredible help to me. Depending on your situation, there are many other types of needs and wants. Open communication is key. Always assume positive intent. The giving person could say, "Please ask me for anything and I will be honest as to whether I am able to help with that project."

Clearly the key is communication and the assumption of positive intent. Sometimes in life, we mean well but just say something in a way that seems unkind when it is really meant to be kind.

Shopping

The shopping part is often hard for someone recovering or home bound. This can result in poor personal care. From your own experience, you could create a list for them by asking if they might need certain items you regularly buy such as dish soap, hand soap, or hand cream. Please encourage them to include things for entertainment. I asked for pretty colored pens. I normally type everything but with my broken wrist I could not type. Therefore, I had to write. An attractive journal notebook and fun colored pens just made writing more interesting and allowed me to organize if I was writing for fun or recording the medical information I needed to capture. A friend of mine found an array of fine point markers and a pretty journal. My sister gave me coloring books, an extensive colored pencil set, and special coloring markers.

The day a person comes home is wonderful for everyone and yet often stressful. There are new supplies that are necessary and often prescriptions or supplements. If you know when the person is coming home, offer to run and gather items or to stay with the person returning home so the caretaker can feel safe in doing such errands. I know when my husband came home from his hip replacement, I was very concerned about leaving him to go buy his prescriptions as well as items temporarily required to provide care like cleansing wipes.

If it is possible, consult with the person prior to the home return day to see if things can be set up in advance. No matter how well we plan, I find that doctors and hospitals always insist on letting you know what you need on the discharge day. This is something I greatly wish medical professionals would change. The best time to prepare for someone coming home is while they are safely being cared for instead of while they are initially at home. It never hurts to ask if you can get prescriptions early—maybe if enough of us ask, they will start to get the idea of how helpful this could be.

In addition, a care package of supplies everyone always needs can never hurt. Items such as tissues, cleaning antibacterial wipes, hand sanitizer (I suggest placing one of these right by the front door for visitors especially if they have medical professionals coming in to care for them), toilet paper, personal toilet moist wipes, personal shower wipes (bathing wipes), paper towels, food zipper storage bags of varying sizes, felt tip permanent marker for food and pills, paper plates, plastic disposable glasses, disposable silverware, and other such items. I will add a caveat here. Some people are against disposable items. When caring for a family or friend, I feel this is the one time to utilize items which help to keep life uncluttered with daily tasks. Not everyone feels as I do. For friends who do not like to use disposable items, it can be helpful to provide things like extra washcloths, cloth napkins, sheets, pillow cases, light blankets, and dishcloths so they are not required to do laundry as often.

Purchasing Personal Items

I found it most helpful to have another person of the same gender ask to buy the personal items. My husband, though willing, had no knowledge of what I might need or where to buy it. Women, please help other women in this area. A friend mentioned how difficult it was when he had to buy personal items for his mother, not because he was unwilling but because women have too many options.

Some personal items which people provided for me were amazingly helpful. When a person is mobile, a bottle of hand sanitizer in the bathroom is sufficient. When a person is stuck in bed or limited in mobility, a pump bottle of hand sanitizer everywhere is more helpful. I exaggerate only slightly. The person does need hand cleaner or hand wipes near where they sit, where they eat, in the bathrooms, in the car, and especially at the entrance for anyone to use as they enter. By the way, always use hand cleaner when you enter the house of someone recovering; no need to bring something contagious into the house for the homebound person whose resistance may, in fact, be limited. Smaller bottles of hand cleaner and individually packaged wipes are perfect for the person's wheel chair, walker, or travel bag as they go out for doctor appointments or physical therapy. The big supply chains have multi-packs of this type of product or the dollar store allows you to buy them for a reasonable price. Once you purchase these items, it could be helpful to place them strategically for the person.

When I was in the hospital for over a month, I wanted things that I never needed at home. I wanted a toothbrush that was nicer than those provided. I wanted a package of toothbrushes so that I could use a new one if one landed on the floor. Some stores sell sets of travel sized toothbrushes, toothpaste, or mouthwash. I also appreciated the toothbrush case a friend found for me. I liked having one of those packages of cheap combs. Let's face it—medical professionals are immune to how icky it is to place personal items on the bed tray after they have used it to hold an unsanitary item.

At home, when bedbound, it can also be nice to have an extra toothbrush and mouthwash next to the bed with a set of disposable cups. When you can't get out of bed or stand for any length of time, you have to be resourceful.

A Need For Different Pants

This is the strange thing—a patient may need clothing or other items that they have never needed before and may be sensitive about asking someone to buy these items. In reality, they may not even know they have options to feel more comfortable. Once they are home anything feels better than that hospital gown. When you have an injury, a cast, or a halo (fixator), clothing can be a challenge.

In my case, I could not wear any of my normal clothes. My right leg, initially wrapped in what looked like plastic wrap attached to a machine by a tube, clearly could not be covered by normal clothing. In addition, I had a seven pound halo holding my leg together from my knee to my ankle that would not permit any normal size pants. My right foot was terribly swollen and impeded by the halo pushing into the swelling with no room for a shoe or slipper between.

A friend immediately went in search of cheap clothes that could have one leg cut off to fit over the halo which was holding my leg together. She found inexpensive five dollar scrubs at a big box store with a tie waistband and big pant legs. To keep things sanitary, you need several changes of clothing or laundry becomes a daily activity.

With the right leg cut off of my pants, my leg was now exposed to the winter cold and hospital germs when I had a doctor's appointment. My sister came to the rescue and made me what I called leg cozies. She made three of them so that my husband did not need to wash them daily. The cozy wrapped around the broken part of my leg to keep it protected and warm during the very cold weather. It was a very simple design though she took it to an advanced level creating a bit of fun. She sewed a flat rectangle with a drawstring top and bottom to gather around the halo and keep it in place. She, being creative, made the leg cozy reversible so that I ended up with six different looks.

My aunt and cousins, noticing my frayed cut off pants, actually had three pairs of comfy pants made for me. These pants were specially designed with velcro up the side of the right leg and several pockets. This was not only helpful at home with my daily leg care but also allowed doctors to access the leg without me needing to change into a medical gown. To this day, when I go to doctor or physical therapy appointments, this velcro design is so very helpful.

Once the halo was removed, I still had a need for special clothing. My injured right leg will never be the same size as my left leg and will always require compression bandages. Once again, a friend to the rescue. This friend gave me patterns for very nice looking pants that have flared flowing legs which will hide the leg size differences and allow me to have a more professional look. She recommended fabrics and off to the store we went to find the perfect options. This provides a professional almost skirt like look with the comfort and flexibility of pants.

These are the types of things to think about when your friends are facing injuries. Do they need looser clothing? My neighbor gave me two pairs of slippery work-out pants that worked perfectly for sleeping since trying to move my bandaged leg was difficult due to the added friction against the sheets. I never would have thought any of these issues existed.

A Need for Different Tops

The leg endured the biggest injury so that must be the end of the clothing story, right? Sorry, I am not a fashion conscious person but clothing, when in rehab and recovering at home, can be a very dramatic concern. I never ever would have guessed.

Simple activities like getting in and out of cars and bed were now extremely difficult and any clothing that could get in the way made it even more challenging. I therefore needed tops that did not go beyond my waist. Anything longer would get caught as I tried to slide into place. A close friend found sport pullover tank tops that were stretchy yet snug and supportive. These allowed me to dress with my broken wrist, prevent tugging as I got into and out of bed, and allow for easier movement as I slept. These were inexpensive and came in packs of three. She bought fun colors to brighten the day.

And though we should not be picky, at times like these, it was wonderful when friends considered my normal wardrobe colors and styles. I have never worn anything brown, tan, cream, or orange in my adult life because I really look worn out in browns—sorry Cleveland football team! Other people look fabulous in these colors and look scary in bright colors. For you men reading this book, it has to do with our skin colors. I really appreciate that my friend knew me well enough to pick blacks, blues, whites, and bright colors. These colors gave a bit of a boost to the day and helped others see me as recovering.

A neighbor, who runs several community projects for her church, also came to my rescue. She worked with a local consignment store to provide clothing to individuals in need through her church mission. Lying in bed, I had no idea how my weight and clothing sizes were going to end up. I did not want to invest a lot of money into clothes that were needed on a short term basis when money was already a concern. She brought over bags of clothes for me to try, and she continued to bring over special items that she knew would make me feel more like my old self.

If you have some clothes in your own closet that might be the right size, don't hesitate to offer. Loaning a person a winter cape or shawl if they are in a cast can really save the day. In my case, being vertically challenged, it was really hard to find tops that were short enough to not be in the way when I would get into bed. I had everyone on the hunt and appreciated all efforts new or borrowed.

↬ It is Not About Vanity

When illness, surgeries, or injuries cause changes in appearance, weight, or body shape, a person has to determine how they want to dress and present themselves. All of us have developed a look throughout our lives whether it be professional, sophisticated, comfortable, casual, or unique. When significant changes occur either to our body or our lifestyle, we may need a new way to create the same image or find a fabulous new self and public image—stronger, braver us.

A new friend who is an image consultant spent hours helping me find clothing options. I could no longer wear fancy shoes to create that "put together" look for business meetings. I did not know how to buy clothing to accommodate the changes to a body that could no longer hike and bike for fitness. I am not a trend conscious person, though I do need to be able to look professional for work.

My new friend gave me amazing guidance on how to create a new image. She went above and beyond the call of friendship. She did not live locally so she sent me photos of clothing options which would look professional. She suggested appropriate colors and very explicit style details. Knowing how hard it was for me to change outfits and the need for me to maintain very sanitary conditions for the care of my leg, she suggested how I could take a tape measure to the store with me and measure clothing instead of needing to try on items.

She provided me with encouraging words about getting out in the work world again without concern for my frumpy men's shoes and more casual attire.

Once the image consultant provided me with the knowledge, I needed to find the time and the energy to go out and implement her recommendations. Once again, friends to the rescue. Friends took me shopping and were very patient as we searched for the items identified by the image consultant. One of my friends altered the sleeve length on a suit jacket that was perfect in every other dimension—we validated this by sending the image consultant a photo. What a world we live in today, we are able to shop in person and use photos to confirm our choice selection.

A Little Self Attention

While lying primarily in bed for nine months, I paid very little attention to my appearance having no energy to do so. Gradually, in a very positive way, friends and family started to encourage me to regain some of my customary routine.

At first I did not have access to a shower and, with my neck injuries, I was not able to place my head in a sink, let alone stand for that much time. My hair was beyond horrible. A close friend devised a way to wash my hair once a week without me needing to get out of bed. We used those inexpensive plastic tablecloths you can buy at any dollar store. One tablecloth went under my upper body and draped over the edge of the bed under a plastic bin on the floor. Another tablecloth cut into a square was placed under my head and brought up around my neck to form a funnel falling over the side of the bed into the bin. We did use extra towels to ensure that water did not escape onto the mattress at any point. Then, she would wash and rinse my hair using a pitcher of water—this did work best when two people were able to work together. Once my hair was washed, the bin was rinsed out and everything was placed inside the bin ready for the next week.

Unable to attend to my hair, it grew down to my waist becoming dried out with the new growth surprisingly gray (who knew) and the ends still my prior colored brown. My family and my friends provided me with creative solutions to have my husband's and my hair cut. My husband's hair specialist came to cut his hair even though this meant an hour drive. My friend's hair specialist came to the house and cut our hair. And my sister-in-law and niece set up their hair person to meet me at their house in order that she might cut my hair. It is surprising how looking more like yourself can help you begin to feel more like yourself. My image consultant friend sent me to her hair salon for a no fuss, no work hair solution that I could wear professionally. I had never liked short hair and initially fought the change. In the end, after I received many compliments and the hair style took no effort, I continue to wear this hair style.

Through my friends' encouragement, I started to gradually take care of my skin again, add some makeup, and put together attractive outfits. This, in conjunction with my new no fuss hair, helped others to see me as my old self instead of seeing me as the bed-confined invalid. Their energy fed my energy to keep up the fight.

Even Feet Need Gentle Care

Another very difficult item for me was shoes. So many friends tried to help. One friend created a shoe store for me at home, bringing multiple sizes of slip-on shoes trying to accommodate one very swollen foot and one normal foot. She then returned them as nothing we could find at the time worked. We found that before the halo was removed the challenge was impossible.

Fortunately, I am now able to wear slippers when I walk within the house and though I used to go barefoot, doctors warn about this with my circulation challenges. The same goes for people with diabetes—protecting the feet is important.

A neighbor bought slippers with soft insides determining that this would allow for the swelling on the injured leg. Slippers with no backs allowed for the different feet dimensions. Another friend took me to a huge shoe store with tons of options where the sales clerk indicated prior experience as a medical aide. The sales clerk worked to solve my shoe challenge. In the end, we determined that I needed to buy two different sizes in the same men's tennis shoes. The left shoe fit normally and the right shoe was worn with the laces wide open.

Other people told me about shoe stores and pharmacies that focused on medical needs with personal assistance and knowledge. Look for stores that specialize in diabetic solutions. The cost associated with custom shoes may not be practical when there is temporary swelling.

We also discovered the stretchy shoe strings which greatly help when you cannot bend over to tie your own shoes. A great shoe kit includes a sturdy long handled shoe horn, the stretchy shoe strings, and big loose socks for inside shoes. I like the grippy socks if walking without shoes though many medical professsions do not feel those are terribly safe for walking as the grippy material can shift.

My pharmacist friend provided me with magnetic insoles. These insoles helped with my circulation, healing, and surprisingly, strength. I found the magnetic insoles to be fabulous for foot and leg nerve pain.

Feet need gentle care also. A dear friend put moisturizer on my feet because they were so horribly dried out. This was a wonderful caring gesture for I could not reach my own feet. During my time in bed, no one told me that it was possible to have a podiatrist come to your house to care for your feet. My husband kindly tried to do what he could carefully do. When he came home from the hospital, we were told about visiting podiatrists by a friend; what a fabulous, caring treatment. I would encourage the doctors to set you up with this type of service if you know you will be house-bound for a long time.

Bundling for Cold Weather

In Ohio, like many other states, the weather fluctuates greatly. Extreme cold and extreme heat can be a definite challenge when you are not able to get into your normal clothing. In bed with the injured leg I discovered normal blankets and sheets were uncomfortable and heavy. Several people made beautiful gifts that warmed me physically and warmed my heart by their loving gestures.

My cousin, who lives far far away, made me an infinity scarf without knowing how helpful it would be to have a scarf without long loose ends that can often drag or get caught. I wore it every time I went out and enjoy its beauty to this day.

A woman we never met—the mother of our neighbor—upon my stay in the hospital immediately sent over a beautiful purple and black single bed quilt and a lovely prayer shawl. Both were the perfect size because I could easily move them, they kept me warm, and they did not tangle. The prayer shawl kept my shoulders warm as I lay in the hospital bed. It is best if family or the person giving the shawl gives it a quick wash in an allergen-free detergent before having someone in a hospital use it.

Another cousin made me a lovely prayer shawl. You might read this and think that I received too many. In reality, during a cold Ohio winter, for a person who cannot wear their normal coat, you can never have too many. In the hospital, having two of anything is perfect so that one can be washed while the other is used. At home, for me it was wonderful to have one to go to doctor's appointments, being able to leave it packed in a carry case ready to grab and use, while the other sat in the recliner ready to provide warmth.

My niece and sister both gave me small fleece blankets. Both of these were again perfect for different locations in the house because small, lightweight, soft, snuggly items were the treasure of the day. It is hard to regulate your temperature when sick and hard to keep from getting tangled when you only have one hand functioning. And since it is often impossible for an injured person to cart a blanket from room to room or chair to chair or house to car, it is great to be able to set up multiple snuggle zones. In addition, cleanliness for some injuries or health issues is key so being able to swap out a warm blanky when another is in the wash can also be very helpful.

Other helpful cold weather ideas include wraps and capes for they do not require buttons and arm placement when arms are broken.

Special Items

If the patient requires something special or medically oriented, you may want to research if there are local stores specializing in medical care items. The next book in this series will be about the help others gave me in navigating the medical world. Look to that book for more on this subject.

My sister made me a beautiful special carry pouch for my walker. It had several pockets for medical records, a book, my phone, my medical card and wallet, a notebook, water, and the all-important snack.

For Christmas, my sister made special wheelchair and phone carry pouches for my husband. She recognized I was juggling too many things when he and I would leave the house. I would end up carrying both cell phones which was not only cumbersome, it meant if he were using his power chair and we would become separated, that he would not have the ability to contact me. The wheelchair bag provided a place to carry a pen, pencil, paper pad, and any literature required at a doctor's appointment or other event.

It is amazing how there are different things you need to carry when you have a physical challenge. I have had to develop multiple go bags to deal with our medical concerns. We carry physical therapy tools to events, to the office and back, to the therapy pool, and to use while riding in the car.

Also drug stores which focus on medical supply items have things like trays for walkers and storage items for crutches.

Cleaning

Many of us think that cleaning has to be the yuckiest thing on the earth to do. Especially those of us with a little OCD behavior where cleaning means washing every crevice. We would never think to ask anyone to do any cleaning for us because that would seem like asking a friend or stranger to go play in a mud puddle. The funny thing is that some people actually like to clean just like some people like to play in mud puddles. If you are one of those people, by all means offer to clean if the person is recovering, even if you feel this is something the spouse can handle. Make sure you let them know that you actually find the task rewarding. In reality, spouses and caretakers can be exhausted just from fighting the medical system on behalf of their loved one. A clean bathroom, though important to healing, may seem overwhelming.

You can also specify what type of cleaning you are open to doing. I did not feel I could ask anyone to clean my bathroom. I really should have had a very sanitary environment yet the bathroom would become unpleasant. One friend stopped to visit and went to use the restroom. She was gone for an extended time. Later I went to the bathroom and discovered she had cleaned it for me. What an amazing surprise!

Another neighbor who is in her 80's offered to come over and clean. I was hesitant—feeling as if I would be imposing. She took the time to assure me that she liked to clean and felt a sense of accomplishment when she was done.

Make sure when you are volunteering to clean that you indicate if you are open to following any special cleaning instructions that people may have. Remember, you never have to offer again if what they ask is not within your ability or preference. Oh, and of course you need to let them know if something is outside of your ability and interest area. I would willingly clean someone's kitchen or run a vacuum. I am not keen about cleaning someone's bathroom.

Who would ever think that cleaning can be a venue of such discussion? Today's chemical cleaners can, in fact, affect some people—I, like many other people, try to use more basic or natural products. Make sure to offer to use the person's cleaning products or to bring ones that you are used to using. Check to make sure about any surfaces requiring special treatment or if they should be avoided. I had to ask that no one clean the front of our fridge—the silly thing scratches if you use even a paper towel on it. I suggest that a conversation is important before starting a project. Allergies and sensitivities to cleaning products could have a negative impact on a person.

A very sweet friend came over before Christmas and helped me do a complete cleaning job of my living room starting with art on the walls on down to moving the furniture and sweeping. My sister even brought her easy-to-handle hand vacuum when she came to take care of me after my skin graft surgery when I was not allowed out of bed for five days. She walked around hitting those areas that get ignored such as cobwebs and corners. Another friend fixed our vacuum when it seemed to stop picking up the dog hair—he could have charged us because it is his business but kindly did it for free.

A fun way to do a deep cleaning might be to get a group together of 3 to 5 people each armed with a bucket (again the dollar stores have these for a buck), rubber gloves, and the homeowner's favorite cleaner. Each person takes a room starting at the top and working to the most dirty— the internet had instructions that popped up one day about cleaning from top to bottom ending with the toilet and floor. Yep, I followed instructions on how to clean to minimize the spread of bacteria. Giving the house a really good spring cleaning no matter the time of year makes it much easier for the caretaker or injured person to maintain a super clean house.

And once again, caring for another is made up of activities that can take a moment to complete to activities that can take days. Carrying a dish into the kitchen before you leave is awesome. When you stop by to visit, let the person know if you are open to running the vacuum or broom as your standard visit task. A wonderful friend of ours would bring her carpet cleaner periodically because, with all the traffic through the house, the carpet would get dirty very quickly. Never feel a need to clean the entire house—it is amazing if you pick a task or a small area and, with the homeowner's permission, go for it.

Another friend would come over weekly and load the dishwasher because dishes tended to pile up. She would also hand wash pots and pans. While she was doing that, I would sort the overflow of containers or cleaning off a cluttered surface—some project that I just had not had time to tackle. Another friend would come over and help me tackle cleaning the refrigerator out—cleaning all the drawers and shelves I was not yet able to lift. We did super fridge cleaning when our basement wall caved in and we had to move out of our house. I imagine the refrigerator would have been ruined without the help I received.

There were just too many chores to get through and I was still barely walking. It was a comfort to have friends who would come over to visit and share in the kitchen chores. It relieved some daily task pressure. And believe it or not, it gave us some quality chatting time because kitchen cleaning does not take a lot of mental concentration.

When I was hit, my husband and I were in the middle of building our new porch and updating many other aspects of our home. I had building and painting supplies everywhere. His family organized and cleaned up many of these areas. I know they cleaned up my painting supplies in the dinette. They organized the garage and the yard where I had been storing our front porch construction supplies. As a result, there was room for the car in the garage. I can only imagine how much time they spent working at the house while I was in the hospital.

The neighbor across the street and the neighbor beside us both hired their personal cleaning people to come over and help for a couple of visits. Both women then offered to continue their cleaning services at what I am sure was a much discounted rate once they saw the health concerns that we were facing.

As we all experience, there are always ongoing daily cleaning needs and then, with special situations, even more extensive cleaning requirements. Offering to help or providing resources that can be trusted can be so very helpful in times of distress.

➳ Never Ending Laundry

Laundry, a bottomless pile that often needs to be addressed daily when people are sick or injured. I was OCD clean when my husband had his hip replacement. I washed the sheets on his chair and bed every day to prevent infection. When they were changing the bandages on my leg, I had to have clean sheets daily. Extra sheets are very helpful. I have found it helpful to cover chairs, car seats, and even the floor when bandaging. I had purchased extra twin sheets at a discount store for his hip replacement. White is great because they can be bleached.

Our family and friends, when visiting, would throw a load of laundry into the washer or fold anything in the dryer. This could be something you offer to do if you are a regular visitor. Or, you can offer to take laundry home as so many of our friends did when our washer broke. Our neighbor across the street told me that with two little ones, she was not able to come over and help, but if she could do anything such as laundry, she would happily take it home. When the washing machine broke, she frequently did several loads for me including running some items through her sanitizing option which takes a really long time. It was hard for me to get out and look for new machines so several friends went well beyond the call of duty and picked up and dropped off folded laundry. Such an amazing and kind gift by all of them. This again is a great time for the person to have extra sheets, towels, and wash cloths on hand. One set is at the laundry while another is being used.

We were blessed by our friends helping us to purchase our new washer. Their daughter worked for a company that specialized in such items. They helped us determine which washing machine to buy, what issues to avoid, and how to get the best price. My sister and brother-in-law also did research for me on potential models. An item such as this is a big ticket item at all times and especially when finances are so strained by the high cost of health issues. Finding time to do all the potential research at a time like this is impossible and, therefore, could result in the risk of a bad decision that one must then live with for years. Sometimes the best gift of support you can give a person during a high stress time is the gift of rational thinking. I am suggesting helping people process and giving them options—I am definitely not suggesting that anyone would want to make the decisions for the person.

When the basement wall collapsed, there was a lot of laundry in baskets and bins on the basement floor. Family, friends, and neighbors once again came to our rescue. First, of course, carrying it all out of the basement and putting it in our garage. Some of the items caked with mud were put on our lawn to get rinsed off by an upcoming rain—unfortunately, I was not able to then get to it quickly enough before the sun faded the items (a warning hint that I never would have thought about). Then family and friends sorted through the bags and bags before they molded. Some more treasured items were taken by people to the laundromat or to their homes. A neighbor took an entire pick-up load to a local dry-cleaner that then proceeded to clean the remainder of the clothing giving us a discount based on the volume. Thank goodness friends and family recognized that these were tasks we could not handle on our own.

I would also suggest laundry services as a potential gift of caring assistance. I know many dry cleaning companies offer drop off and pick up services. Our cousin who cared for her mother used such a service for her husband's work clothing in order to ensure he always had the required clothing if she were to be distracted by a medical emergency.

Plants Need Care to Live

We never thought about who would provide the required care for our plants or furry children should something happen. I am fortunately not a big inside plant person—well, I need to correct that because over the winter I work very hard to keep several of my outside plants alive in order to adorn the porch over the summer. Most of my plants resided upstairs where I was not able to go. A friend of mine, who had been my friend since junior high, came over frequently and helped with so many things. She is very organized and realized there were plants upstairs needing tender care.

It would be easy to say "Oh well, they are just plants." At the time you just don't care. As you feel better, if you let the plants die, it would become another loss to get over. And I would try to avoid comments such as "They're only plants," "You have more important things to worry about," etc. The plants may have been a gift or have sentimental value—many people have plants in memory of a loved one. If there is no one to care for them, then yes, gently help the person move forward and accept any plant loss. As friends, try whenever possible to reduce any additional loss. Periodically, ask the friend how they are feeling and listen with compassion, not judgment. Please refrain from telling a person how they should feel!

I am grateful to everyone who worked so hard to maintain our life, adding so much additional work to their own lives as a result. My high school friend brought over clean shoes to wear upstairs, knowing that before this happened and still today, I never wear dirty street shoes upstairs. Each week, she went upstairs and cared for the plants—they thrived under her attention! Because of her, the plants were here to be enjoyed once I resumed the responsibility.

My husband, mom, and sister took the outside plants and kept as many of them alive as was possible. My mom and sister took clippings that they rooted in water to try to ensure special varieties survived. When my sister's clippings did not survive, she found seeds of special varieties and started several dozen that I could grow the next summer. She and my mom came to my house and filled the summer pots with dirt and her seedlings. The plants my husband took to his office flourished under his care with the artificial lighting, big picture windows, and constant attention. His assistant stepped in and kept them watered if he needed to be home with me for an extended period of time.

My friend read the directions on new plants that were given to me and took care of them as was instructed. She took plants that were bulbs home with her to store for the winter. She regularly watered, trimmed, and separated items as was needed. I know that I never cared for my own plants as well as she did.

Years ago when my house was being remodeled, a friend took my plants home with her and cared for them at her own house. My sister had her friend's plants at her home one year when her friend was not able to care for them. So even if you cannot consistently care for something at the injured person's home, maybe you can take items with you that you can then give back later when they are better. And this can be a great help because with all the additional medical care equipment, having the items out of the house can also be a big help.

The moral of this story: The care of living or non-living items that are special to a person is a kindness that is remembered well after any injury or recovery. Because of the assistance friends provided us, I was able to enjoy items that would have died during my time in bed. Another lesson is that had these friends not taken care of my plants there would no longer be plants to enjoy, so I never would have wanted anyone to worry while the plants were under their care.

Outside Chores

Depending on the time of year, the person might need help with regular outside chores such as leaf removal, snow removal, mowing, or weeding. Depending on whether the care concern was planned (for example my husband's hip surgery the month before I was hit) or due to an emergency (my being hit in the post office, the basement wall collapsing, or my husband's stroke) will determine if the person was able to prepare to have these items handled during their recovery. For long term concerns, it would make sense to help the person find a paid resource to handle the tasks at hand. Though if seeking paid resources, it might be an option to consider a fundraiser because finances clearly can become strained when unexpected health issues occur. For short term concerns, this could be handled like the cleaning effort—by one person once or a team of people to cover a certain period of time.

Prior to the injury, I created a new attractive flower bed to hold my vast collection of daylilies and to complement the size of our new porch. I tried to design something with limited care needs though I felt that I would enjoy keeping up with the garden during the pleasant summer weather. Unfortunately, the design required more than minimal care. And due to my injuries, my doctor really does not want me doing yard work—in fact one doctor asked if I really needed to be outside at all. While visiting my husband in the hospitals and managing the basement wall replacement process, the thistles and other weeds took over the garden.

The first challenge was that I was just finalizing the garden when I was hit by the car. I had been clearing a section while taking care of my husband after his hip replacement. I had the ground all prepared and a big bucket of bulbs that needed to be planted. Our niece volunteered to finish the job. She carefully planted the bulbs so that we did not lose them after I had put so much work into digging them out of other gardens that spring. This made me feel so much better that all the hard work I had done did not go to waste. Then once spring came, her work gave us that boost of energy which always happens when spring flowers make their joyous appearance.

The first summer, my mom, sister, and a friend worked together to keep the weeds at bay. The next year, a group from our church cleared the weeds and added wood chips. The following year a couple we know came multiple times to once again try to gain some thistle control. The thistles were my height and once pulled filled every trash can and bin we could find. A young neighbor helped me get all the containers to the curb for trash day. And then once again my mom and sister helped me to periodically regain control. Now we have a friend who we hired to keep the garden weeds under control with a strategy to change the garden design in such a way as to require less future care and maintenance. Without their help, the front garden would look like the backyard looked after the basement reconstruction—an absolute disaster.

Recently, family friends came over and attacked everything that had been neglected throughout the entire yard. They moved at a rapid pace using the weedwacker and removing items that had been left behind from the basement project. A pile of trash ended up at the curb and a pile of brush ended up in the woods. It is now pleasant to look out back instead of a sad reminder of the year's events. It is amazing how when people complete these projects it not only checks a chore off the list; but more importantly, provides a sense of peace. The yard projects can sadly be a constant reminder of abilities lost. The positive input and energy created by the kindness of others replaces the sadness with energy and determination.

My brother-in-law installed a ramp for my husband in order for him to return home from rehab. The ramp was outside and exposed to the rain, ice, and snow. I covered the ramp with painting tarps to protect it from the elements. They were then easily removed for a safe, slip-free, dry surface. We used a lot of natural ice melt because it is safe for humans, pets, and plants—a wonderful gift idea. I always bought some each year and delivered it to my mom—a task I sadly have not been able to do since my injuries.

In cold climates, the chores change throughout the year. During the winter, two neighbors kept the driveway and walk cleared of snow. Our neighbor, who had just bought a new snow blower, would often come every hour during a snow storm. Several people also helped me shovel the sidewalk to the house.

Then my husband's friend started plowing the driveway without letting us know. I came home one day and it was cleared. I stood looking at the driveway with my head tilted, just as my dog does, trying to figure out how the driveway had been cleared. No snow was sprayed onto the lawn as appears with a snowblower. I thanked a neighbor who responded that he had not done it. During the next snow storm my husband heard a sound and we caught another friend in action. He was plowing the driveway. These friends gave us such reassurance knowing the big driveway job would be done for us. It was hard enough for me to keep the porch and sidewalk cleared!

Our friends who would drive my husband to work would also help at times with the snow removal. I would try to have it done before they would arrive, but some mornings just don't go the way you plan no matter how early you try to start. I can't remember the number of times they either cleared the path to the car or cleared more of the driveway before taking my husband off to work. We then finished the job with the pet-safe driveway melt to ensure a safe journey for everyone.

Any knowledge you have regarding how an injured person might be able to stay safe when conditions are dangerous would be great to share. My sister found non-skid shoe attachments at a local department store that attach to shoes reducing the slip risks. She also suggested mats that are supposed to prevent ice build up though I have not found them yet. I am sure others have incredible ideas that I have never even thought about.

Winter can be a very dangerous time outside for a sick or injured person. If you live nearby, offer to take the trash to the curb when you take out your own. Our neighbor across the street would kindly take mine to the curb when the snow made it to difficult for me. A neighbor would often bring our paper up to the porch to save us a trip to the mailbox. This is especially important if you see a paper on the driveway as the snow is starting to come down because it actually could cause the homeowner to slip or it could really jam up an unsuspecting snowblower. Items like this take a moment for a healthy person but can take considerable time or add considerable risk to an injured person. If the person has multiple exit doors you may want to call or send a text letting them know their paper is now on their front porch or by a specific door so they do not go looking for it. We have a front porch and only use that door so it was easy to see our paper had been personally delivered. If this is something that happens frequently then you might want to offer setting up a waterproof decorative mailbox or container near the door for you to place the mail and paper.

Years ago I was going through a difficult time. I enjoyed getting outside to just get some exercise and have some time to think. That season, I kept about five neighborhood front yards cleared of leaves. It just felt good to be outside and I knew it was appreciated. No one asked me to do it. I just wanted to surprise them periodically with a break and thank them for being such good friends. Sometimes when you are set up to do a task, it can take only a few minutes to extend that task to someone close to you.

Carpentry and Repair

I am going to leave this one as quite obvious. If you have the talent to help a person safely and securely install the necessary equipment or make the necessary changes to a house, offer your time. You can attempt to find material for them, keeping a separate receipt for the family to reimburse you. If you have the ability to design outside the box and the changes are extremely safe, then offer suggestions.

Check into temporary or portable ramps if that would be adequate, again ensuring safety for the necessary duration. One must make sure codes are followed for safety purposes.

For the bathroom, I worked with the occupational therapists to find a safe solution. Fortunately I was persistent. It took me four different occupational therapists before I gained help in designing a railing out of plumbing for our half bathroom. The design mimicked what the industry calls a standing frame allowing the location to serve as a therapy option and as a means for access to all bathroom fixtures. If I had not pushed for some type of design solution they would have insisted on a bedside commode which would have completely reduced the therapy aspect and increased the patient risk.

In addition, there may be projects the person was already doing when they were injured. In our case, we had several projects underway.

I was working in the basement and had most of our clothing and many of our treasures spread out everywhere. My mother and sister packed up things as best they could so they would not be lying around on the floor. It took two of them over an hour to complete.

I was in the middle of replacing the caulking in our master shower. Two friends worked on finalizing the caulk removal and then replaced it for me so the shower was once again usable. I am not able to bend down anymore and do not know what I would have done without their help.

The weekend before my husband had his hip replacement, we spent the entire weekend sanding and sealing our front porch floor. The finish had not dried sufficiently to replace all of the furnishings so friends helped me return the heavier items to the porch.

I was in the middle of many projects. I had set up shelves in the dinette to store what I needed at the time. While I was in the hospital, family members cleaned up my work area to ensure better access to the back of the house through the dinette.

Whether the person is in the middle of projects or not, there is always something that needs to be done around the house to either ensure a safer environment or to make repairs. Offering help or referring trusted resources can ease a person's concerns.

Let There Be Light

You are thinking that I am going to discuss some motivational topic about hope within this section, aren't you? Nope. I really mean, let there be light. You would not believe how important light becomes when you are injured or sick. Normally, we have lamps on our bedside tables. And normally, we don't care if we feel around in the dark to get to a light switch. Yet when we are injured or sick, these previous normal set-ups need new solutions. I was too weak to reach the lamp switch. I was terrified of tripping on the way to the bathroom if the room was dark. Though I am sure this topic could fill its own book, I feel highlighting the solutions people devised for my benefit will give you plenty of your own ideas.

When I was sleeping on a daybed placed in the living room, I had to keep the hall lights on or the dining room lights on so I could safely use my walker to get to the bathroom. And the only thing I could do during the middle of the night when I could not sleep was watch TV because I did not have sufficient light to read or write. New and improved lighting solutions helped me be safe and helped me relax.

A dear friend had an extra book light which she brought for me and we clipped it onto the back of the daybed. This allowed me at night to read and write—thus the start of this book. It also gave me a source of light to find anything that I needed which I kept within reach.

Another friend provided a night light that is triggered based on the level of light in the room, guaranteeing that I would have light to guide my way to the bathroom. And since there is no outlet in our hallway, it was perfect that it was battery operated.

A friend picked up a lantern so that the room could be illuminated without electricity when our power went out or while our house was empty from the basement wall disaster. It gave the appearance of someone being home while we were evacuated.

In addition, simple life tasks are no longer simple. I never previously thought about what it takes to change a light bulb. Did you know it is not possible for someone with a broken wrist and an injured leg to change the light bulbs for overhead lights? Without help, they just kept burning out. So over a few months the lighting became insufficient, unsafe, and dreary. A friend brought light bulbs and replaced the bulbs in the downstairs light fixtures. It was suggested that we invest in long lasting light bulb technology since changing light bulbs will continue to be a challenge. Plus she mentioned the energy-saving benefits.

At Christmas time I made a discovery—our Christmas tree remote! Dah! Why not plug the lamp next to the couch into the Christmas tree remote and then use the handheld remote to turn the lighting on and off. This has worked brilliantly!

My sister, who lives far far away, looked into sun lamps since we were trapped at home during the darkest months of the year. Research shows that the winter darkness can have an impact on our mood. She watched for specials, and we were able to pick one up using a 60% off coupon at a nearby store. Bright light in a previously dark room makes it so much better when trying to do paperwork or complete a project. And for us, it just enhances our mood.

One night while I was in the middle of helping my husband, the entire house suddenly went pitch black. We both froze. What to do? How to safely get to the flashlight? Where had I left the walker and where was the dog lying so that I did not injure myself?

Fortunately, the lights returned in only a few moments so we remained safe. This inspired me to find lighting that can be used when the power goes out—and I started to pay attention to the commercials for regular light bulbs that will in fact turn on if the power is out.

Or, another option, battery-operated lights can be kept in strategic locations such as the bathroom.

And, does everyone know that some cell phones actually have flashlight options? Or if they know it, do they have the presence of mind to remember such a feature during a stressful time or is it something worth mentioning just in case?

My sister was researching generators so I asked her for the information. If you have experience in this area definitely share your knowledge. When one has serious medical or safety needs, it might be a great idea to have a fundraiser designed to provide a generator attached to the house that does not require monthly maintenance by the homeowner.

So in fact, *Let There Be Light,* is about how important lighting is when one is healing. And the fact that we assume there will always be electricity to provide the necessary lighting is, in fact, not a reality.

Computer Technology

This seems like a strange subject because one assumes that everyone has the technology that they want in place so why would they need technological help? The reality is that health circumstances can in fact change technology desires and needs. Why, you ask? Allow me to share a few scenarios with the realization that there are many others.

In my case, there were several reasons why the current technology set-up I had was not effective once I was injured. First, my left arm was broken so I could not hold the heavy laptop. Second, I was trapped in bed with a severely injured leg so I had no place to rest any type of technology. And finally, while in the hospital I really did not want my phone or computer to be dropped on the hospital floor or be stolen.

My sisters' families purchased an inexpensive tiny computer for me to use at the hospital so that I did not fear someone stealing or breaking any expensive items that might be brought from home. My sisters made a quilted bag that could attach to the side of the bed and hang the computer easily within my reach. My techy wiz of a nephew took considerable care to not only load and set up the computer—he wrote specific step-by-step instructions on how I could use the computer. He loaded videos of my niece's plays that I had missed attending, giving me options to enjoy. The time they all took to do this was incredibly special to me. And my nephew was always kind in getting back to me and answering my questions so that in my confused state I could still move forward.

When my husband was in the hospital, my friend loaned me a computer because I needed specific software that I did not have for a work assignment. An amazing kindness!

Another friend came over and hooked up a very inexpensive wireless printer so that I was able to print from bed since I could not sit at my desk upstairs. I paid $30 for the printer. This made a huge difference.

In my husband's situation, he loves to listen to music on his iPAD—again the huge concern of something happening to it while he was in a rehab facility. I put out the word and two friends came up with iPODS that they were no longer using which could be used to load his music for him to listen. What an amazing solution! Music can be so very healing but some of us know nothing about loading and transferring it.

Technology Technology

So, if technology is an area of enjoyment and strength for you, maybe this is your outreach gift to the person in need. Or maybe a well-stated request to a group of friends could solve numerous technology issues a person might face during a health concern time.

Some reasons technology needs may now be different from before:

- A broken or non-working arm or hand might mean the person could greatly benefit from dictation software and a microphone.
- The location the person is staying might mean expensive equipment is at risk of damage or loss so the person would benefit from finding used equipment or cheaper alternatives.

- The person may not have needed technology at home before and could be better entertained by having some now.
- The person may have never learned how to watch shows on the computer and play video or other games to be entertained.
- The work environment for the patient may have had all the equipment needed, and by providing a new technology set-up, the person may be able to stay more active by working from home.
- The person's primary entertainment may now be television. Does the person have a DVR, a working remote, or a DVD player?

So, if technology is your thing—maybe this is a great way to know the patient better. Maybe the person would benefit from:

- Learning a new game
- Watching a TV show or listening to books on tape
- Researching answers to questions while recovering
- Accessing medical records online
- Keeping in contact with the world via phone or internet technologies
- Working from home or the hospital

Does the person need the technology moved to a different room or a different type of desk? Maybe the computer needs to be on a table that has room for a wheelchair or a new chair is needed to offer sufficient support.

A friend of ours hooked up a humungous TV given to us by a neighbor who was moving. It is awesome because we are no longer able to go to movies. The TV is absolutely too large for the room yet, since it is now a major part of our entertainment, it is fantastic! The neighbor simply had his movers walk it across the street and set it up. Our friend then found us a DVD player and audio system combination at an incredible discount. He then installed everything. Before being injured I barely watched TV. Now when I cannot sleep, I am able to watch things that I previously recorded.

When our friends delivered the DVD player, they also brought a movie they knew we thoroughly enjoyed. Our brother-in-law, niece, nephew, and neighbor also contributed to the movie library for us to enjoy sharing their personal favorite movies. If you have a collection of movies or can stop at the library to find interesting movies, definitely check with the person to see if they are interested. Remember, they are probably stressed and possibly disorganized by all the changes. I know I appreciated the gentle reminders to return the movies or the timely effort by my friends to return items to the library. This is such a relief for people trying to juggle things that they never had to juggle before.

I did a similar thing for a friend years earlier. He had been involved in a tragic accident and had to spend a month in bed. He had a basic television without cable. I had a (now don't judge) VCR that I had used for work programs and a ton of movies to go with it. At that time a lot of his other friends had VCR compatible movies also. We set up the VCR for him to use providing some diverse entertainment. Sometimes it does not even need to be the latest technology—he simply needed something basic to be able to keep him entertained.

My technology knowledge is limited so I leave the possibilities in the hands of the technologically adept. If you have this area of expertise, talk to the person and see if you can offer some guidance and full fledged help.

Phone Technology

It is hard for a person to feel connected when not feeling well. Having a phone to use can be very important. And of course it can be a significant safety issue. I was able to call my husband if I needed him when he was upstairs or outside.

Throughout this time our situation demanded we revise our phone solution. I did not want my expensive phone to be at risk of being broken or stolen. In the hospital, our solution was for me to switch phones with my husband. He had an outdated flip phone that was almost indestructible. Another solution would have been for someone to donate an old phone after ensuring that it could be activated. Check with the family to determine if there are any contract restrictions or ramifications. Another alternative is to purchase an inexpensive phone using a minute by minute plan. I am sure there are many options that I am unaware even exist. Be creative and ask a bunch of questions.

Once I had a phone I needed a carry bag or waist holder to keep track of my phone so it did not fall off the bed. Also, I had my husband scope out a way to attach the phone cord to the bedside table for easy charging access. My sister made my husband a phone carrier that hung around his neck so that he could easily take his phone with him.

As you can tell, it takes time to research and set up a positive solution. While I was restricted to bed, I called the cell phone companies every few days and asked for the best deal until I found a person who actually researched my best option. I literally had nine different answers over a month. I had friends telling me their plans which then gave me questions to ask. I ended up signing up for a cheaper plan with a free smart phone that allowed me to access email and the internet at a time when using the computer was extremely difficult due to my broken wrist.

It turns out at one facility the bedside table was supposed to have a lock. Unfortunately, no one told us for the first two weeks. Though even with a drawer lock, be very careful what you keep with the patient because theft is a really big problem at most medical facilities. There are just too many people in and out so when the patient has to leave the room for tests or therapy you just don't know who is in the room.

Once I returned home, technology still had its challenges because I was confined to the daybed in the living room. Whether confined to bed or hanging out in a recliner unable to easily move, it is very difficult to access everything you need. It was very helpful that a sturdy small table was set up next to the bed with a container for things that needed to be kept safe and easily moved out of the way. The computer and phone charging cords were attached to the bed so that I could reach them. It is so important that there are ways to easily store and access the phone because you don't want a patient hurting themselves trying to reach for a phone when it is critically needed.

Administrative Support

Being sick or injured is like starting a business while you are exhausted and distracted. Your focus should be on healing. You should be getting enough sleep, eating right, doing your therapies, and researching medical solutions.

Instead, the paperwork is overwhelming and inaccurate. Everyone wants to blame the insurance companies. Don't. The entire system has strengths and weaknesses. And the stress it causes is detrimental to healing.

There are numerous ways to help with the administrative process for a patient. I do not think that your prior relationship matters as much as discussing clear privacy boundaries. What would they like help doing? What do they not want shared? Stay away from account numbers, passwords, and social security numbers.

This topic will be discussed in much greater depth in a future book. Under normal circumstances you know that paperwork builds up. When you are sick, it is insurmountable. Any help you can give a person in organizing medical records, bills, or medical supplies may be a gift that you cannot even imagine.

Regular Bill Payments

Daily tasks that are not normally a challenge can become a challenge for the family dealing with a tragedy. The amount of paper that comes into your house during these times is overwhelming. The fact that your house may be disrupted makes it difficult to keep things organized. Some days you may be at the hospital all day and barely getting any sleep. This makes keeping up with all the bills very frustrating.

I remember one time when our friend lost a loved one that we went to their house and paid their bills for which they later reimbursed us. Of course, that is only something you can do with someone you know really well and are certain they will be able to pay you back.

A friend handled many of our monthly household bills. We changed the mailing address to her house. Our monthly bills were fairly consistent so we would write a check to her, and she would make sure those household bills were paid, giving us a summary each month. This reduced the stress, ensured our credit was kept in good standing, and guaranteed the house had lighting and heat. It also freed us up to deal with the numerous new bills now arriving each week.

As the medical bills and basement cave-in bills piled up, some friends who love to organize would process our mail. One would gather our mail and sort it into several attractive boxes we placed on the table. Another friend then took those piles of mail home, opened them, sorted them into a file box, and provided a summary page of what needed to be paid. She creating a separate file for "handle immediately."

If you are knowledgeable about online services for bill paying and banking, you may be able to help the person set up their accounts if they are interested. Always look away when they enter their passwords and social security numbers—it is important to keep such items confidential.

Blessed Again And Again

Traumatic events and tragedies create emotional and physical turmoil whether from injuries, health concerns, world events, or weather events. The world events and weather events are tricky because they often impact numerous people within one community at the same time, making it challenging to help everyone at once. I learned the organizations who advertise assistance during emergency situations may not be responsive when needed because they do not, in fact, have the resources to support multiple catastrophes at once. I learned this the hard way. The majority of our basement back wall completely collapsed due to extreme ground saturation. A two-story house was basically suspended between two visually intact but weakened foundation corners. Though the house was at risk of falling into the mud, I could not find an emergency company to assist us in our time of need.

Without the help of family, friends, and neighbors, once again I know that we would no longer have a house as it would have not been able to hold itself in place without its full foundation for long. In reality, I am sure I could write an entire book focused on this topic. At this time, I am going to highlight a few of the numerous treasured moments that we experienced.

Housing, housing, and housing! Immediate emergency housing for a family, especially a family with a pet, is obviously the first consideration—most hotels do not work, and with my leg, I was also worried about the cleanliness and ease of access within a hotel environment. A friend immediately tried to get through all the flooded streets to come help us as I was still barely walking. She rearranged the sleeping accommodations in her house to provide a place for us to sleep the first night. This included a place for our dog who was not familiar with her many pets—I don't know if our dog even knew what a cat was! Our friend's sweet daughter quickly set up her room for us to use, moving her stuffed animals and changing the sheets. Despite the late hour, they really made us feel safe.

The next day, another family offered us more permanent housing while the repairs were being done. They shared the use of their first floor mother-in-law suite which included a walk-in shower I would be able to access. They opened their entire home to us for as long as it took to get the house somewhat functional again. The room was set up with its own washer and dryer which enabled me to keep up with my bandaging materials and the minimal clothing we were able to bring with us for the stay. This feature would not have existed in a hotel, increasing the risk of infection to my leg.

Once again my brother-in-law and sister-in-law came to the rescue and picked up our "furry child" to live with them for the repair duration. I am sure our "furry girl" felt as if her stay at her own home had been more like a brief vacation since she had only been back home with us for a very short time.

A mason friend took charge of stabilizing our home by renting a pump to pump out the basement, bracing the structure, digging out the basement, and rebuilding the walls. He had much help along the way from family and friends. Our nephew came the first night. The two of them braced the structure, slipping and sliding in the muddy, dangerous rubble.

Our mason hired a team to empty the basement of our belongings and the rubble that once was our wall. They worked as a team with our friends to reduce the emotional impact by having the men carry items to the driveway. Several more friends then processed through the bins and bags to find any items that could potentially be salvaged. They pulled up a chair and insisted that I sit and guide the process. At the time this was very emotionally and physically difficult. Not only was I sitting, unable to help them do the work, but also because I had to decide quickly whether to keep an item covered in mud or whether the item—and the memory I associated it with—should be tossed.

My friends tried to rescue as many memories as possible by carefully cleaning a box of photos, setting aside childhood toys, saving a few of the many Christmas ornaments filled with muddy water, and placing many items in the garage for later consideration. These friends had visited our home at the holidays and had seen the trees fully decorated adorning every single room of the house! I had already experienced so much loss with no longer being able to do the things I loved to do. Our friends were doing everything possible to reduce the loss of personal memories.

My husband ordered and picked up hamburgers from a local restaurant for the crew in order to thank them all—and to keep everyone from passing out from lack of nutrition. We all needed a break and sustenance so his consideration was greatly appreciated. The amount of work was so overwhelming we were afraid they would forget to eat and hydrate.

Time ran out as darkness set in and the dumpster and garage were full. A final push to get the remaining items cleared from the basement created a huge mound on the yard. Over the next week, my friend and a neighbor boy helped me go through the big pile on the yard, trying to see if anything else could be rescued and placing the remaining trash into the new dumpster that arrived. My mother and sister came multiple times to sort through clothing items in the garage and to take home items that might possibly be rescued.

The continued clean-up was only possible with the help of others. My sister's family came twice to work on cleaning items placed in the garage. My brother-in-law and nephew carried, washed, and sorted items and then sorted more items. My niece cleaned jewelry and small treasured items, thoughtfully trying to salvage anything possible. My sister sat for hours cleaning any unbroken dishes that were found in my basement kitchen. My brother-in-law made certain everyone was fed and hydrated.

Once again, without even the potential of a professsional company coming to my aide, the support of family and friends saved—I mean SAVED the day! Friends gave me ideas of contractors to call. The neighbor kept an eye on our house letting us know if there was anyone unfamiliar on our property. Friends and relatives came throughout the first week to clean out the refrigerator and freezer. A friend also installed a lock on the basement door now that there was a gaping hole in our basement. A friend bought a battery operated light so that we could make it look as if someone was inside at night even though there was no electricity to the house.

We would not have had a house in which to live without the help of family and friends. I believe we often expect the professionals to handle everything and I truly would have loved for that to have been the case. It is my suggestion that community organizations have a plan on how to help fellow citizens when events happen to multiple homes at the same time. Prior to my husband having to focus on my care, he was heavily active in caring about the community. He would have inspired fundraisers or community teams to rally around and help those going through difficult times. We are all subject to times of potential crises from many directions—even things as simple as a major electrical trunk line being cut during construction could cause major community disruption. I would hope this guide inspires community groups to have a strategy for helping total strangers during unforeseen, yet widespread events when the individuals, who normally would like to help others, may instead need to focus on their own calamities.

Family Support

When there is a healthy family member, we generally feel they have things under control. And in reality, they may. Each family is different in what they normally juggle. We often do not know that one person has parents or other family members to whom they generally attend, or a child or other family member who requires additional consideration. There are stresses on our friends and family members that we sometimes are not even aware exist for they have no interest in burdening others. I know people who are very private about their own health concerns.

Some families we know both work and often have the support of a grandparent or other individual to assist in their normal healthy daily existence. When one person is taken out of the equation, then there is a gap which needs support.

Family members experience lack of sleep and considerable stress. How can we relieve the stress of the family members? This topic I am sure could be a book on its own. Clearly by helping provide for the patient we are helping the family. In addition, what needs exist within the family?

What normal life activities and commitments are the family members continuing to enjoy? How much of their time is required to care for the sick or injured family member depends on the situation.

In our case, it was incredibly supportive to me when individuals offered to provide transportation for my husband's aide who did not drive—I was fearful to leave my husband unattended. A couple of friends created a regular schedule to provide transportation on specific days. This allowed me to have a plan in place. They even started to communicate directly with each other to ensure I was not required to be in the middle of the daily planning.

A friend found a very sweet person to keep my husband company and ensure his safety so I could participate in the women's Christmas tea at church. I went and was able to relax and enjoy the entertainment without watching the clock and holding onto my phone.

Friends offered to stay with my husband so I could participate in a previously planned theatre event or an outing with friends. I was rarely away from my husband and these opportunities to leave without concern were a definite stress relief.

Even when I was in the hospital or my husband was in the hospital, we really appreciated the friends who came to stay with us when the other spouse could not be there. Even though there are hospital personnel to ensure safety, for us, we greatly appreciated the distraction and entertainment of a friend keeping us company instead of being alone.

Kid Running

Many of us would assume the spouse would be able to handle taking care of the kids. And I am certain the spouse would figure it out, though in the end it may exhaust them and stretch them too far to be fully effective. In many households these days, it takes both spouses to get multiple children to different places. I cannot mention this enough. Everyone in the household is probably very stressed if a loved one is in crisis or even almost in crisis. Therefore, it may be harder at this time to be able to just drop everything to do one's chauffeur role. What if the family member needs therapy or medicine at the same time a child needs to be across town?

There are multiple ways of helping in this situation and not all of them involve driving.

One is to offer to take the kids places. And once again, it is beneficial to indicate preferences. It is great to offer something such as, "I have Wednesdays off and that is when I do my errands. If the kids need to be dropped off and picked up locally on any Wednesday, I would gladly take a break and enjoy their company while driving them to an event. I would need to be able to help for an event with a clear start and end time for I would not be able to stay." Or, "I would love to take them to one of their sporting events and would enjoy staying to watch."

Another way to help is to sit down with a calendar. If they don't already have a multi-line calendar, you could pick one up cheaply at a local discount store. Then you could sit down with a family member and schedule anyone who has volunteered for driving including their phone number. That way the family, including any age-appropriate children, could call the drivers the day before to confirm everyone has remembered times and locations.

And of course, depending on the situation, a third alternative is to offer to stay with the sick or injured family member so the others may attend a child's event without worrying about food or medication for the injured person.

As you can tell, this is all about creativity and sometimes just helping with organization. The family members have systems in place when everyone is well. People become flustered when change happens, especially when that change involves a loved one.

Pet Care and Running

Pets are a very important part of our lives. And the care of our pets is a major concern as we work through difficult events at a time when we may not be able to provide the same level of care as we did previously. During this time, our dog provided the loving support only animals can share with us every day—that unconditional love which nurtures us as we find our way. Therefore, doing everything possible to keep a person and their pets together is something that I, as a major pet lover, feel very strongly about.

We were watching our brother-in-law's dog when I was hit. My brother-in-law and sister-in-law ended their trip early and came and got not only their dog but also our dog immediately. Fortunately, they had watched our beloved dog when we had traveled on vacation so she was right at home. The two dogs knew each other and were fine living in the same house, though at the beginning were truly not friends. They kept our dog for many months, bringing her to visit me a few times. As time went on, my sister-in-law would send me photos or share stories with me about the developing friendship between the two animals and also stories about how our dog was becoming more at home. They always made us feel assured that she was very welcome and very loved.

We brought our furry baby home for only a few months before our basement wall caved in and then back to their house she went. Thank goodness she considered it her second home. I don't know what we would have done otherwise. And of course, she told us how much fun she had staying with them. Every time we went for a visit, she became very excited as we pulled in the driveway, running into the house to greet everyone and making herself completely at home. She still enjoys heading out for a walk with my brother-in-law when we spend time at their house.

Once the wall was fixed and she was able to come home again, my husband immediately went into the hospital. I was still barely able to walk and definitely not strong enough to hold onto a dog when she would pull on her leash. Plus, I was very busy going to the hospital and working as much as I could fit into the schedule. As a result of the constant upheaval in our life, our well-trained dog was acting out and not listening. She would try to get me to chase her down the sidewalk—she wanted to take me for a walk, staying just out of range. She refused to come back in when called.

I put out the word through our church news that I really could use some help if anyone was able to walk a young dog with extra pent up stress energy. It was such a blessing to have a member of our church walk her several times a week, even on cold blustery days. And not only did the person provide our dog with a stress break, he also provided me with a stress break by stopping to chat—sharing stories of others he knew who recovered from difficult injuries or illnesses. He was very kind and would check in to see how we were doing or if I needed any assistance. He walked our pup while my husband was in the hospital and rehabilitation centers.

We were then blessed when a neighbor from down the street, whom we knew from neighborhood events, was walking past and stopped to chat. I mentioned how much our dog missed her walks. Our neighbor amazingly asked if our dog would like to walk with her and her husband. Usually four times a week, they have consistently walked her since. You really can tell the difference in our best friend when she gets out for her exercise. And again, we have gotten to know two wonderful people through this experience. Our dog loves them and whines with excitement when she sees them coming down the road to take her for her walk. We enjoy our opportunities to get to know them better and greatly appreciate their kindness.

So whether it is a cat who needs a lap to sit on for an hour a day or a dog that needs a walk, helping people care for their pets while recovering is so very important in order for them to keep these inspirational creatures.

Other ways to help include creating safe environments for the injured party and the pet. Another brother-in-law set up a temporary fence for our dog so that I did not need to risk slipping on ice during the winter. The fence area allowed me to open the front door so she could safely go out on her own. Sometimes safety features need to be set up inside the house such as doggie gates to prevent tripping over the pet.

And sometimes a person simply needs help getting the pet's food, either due to transportation limitations or weight limitations. The store where I buy our dog food carries the bag out to my car. A friend or neighbor carries the bag into the house. And then I bought a wheeled food container for the food storage. Food supply problem solved.

If you are a pet person and would like to help during a person's recovery, there are the good jobs and the less pleasant chores that a person may temporarily not be able to complete. Litter box and yard clean-up might be a couple chores that may not be safe for a person while they recover. Animal bathing or pet visits are other areas which often require a level of movement that might temporarily not be possible. Or if it is a longer challenge, a wonderful gift idea would be to buy an automatic litter box, gift certificates to a groomer, or gift certificates to a doggie daycare.

Some people would say that it is then time for the person to find a new home for their furry companion. And if the injuries are going to present life-long challenges, then helping to find a good home may be the necessary option. Research shows our furry friends offer stress relief and comfort. Therefore, if there is a way to keep an animal with their owner, I strongly feel it is the best alternative. And there are so many resources available these days which can make it possible.

Adult Companionship

In both my husband's and my situations, the companionship provided by family and friends was both energizing and critical for our safety. Both of us needed 24/7 care for months after we first came home. The only way the caretaker was able to leave without worrying was to have someone at home with the injured spouse. Several of the people who came to stay with me started out as acquaintances and have transitioned to close friends.

Several family members and friends volunteered to come and stay with me so my husband could go to work. Most people brought lunch, ensuring enticing foods to keep me eating at a time of limited appetite. Many people had unique ideas on activities to do or encouraged me to stand or walk during part of their visit. This was a great way to spend part of the time because once people left I was often tired and needed to sleep. Sometimes people helped me sort and store the endless pile of medical supplies that arrived regularly or the mounting stacks of medical paper-work. People brought organization containers or my cousin organized the supply boxes in what looked like a stacking cube set to ensure easy access.

Our minister came to visit weekly no matter where I was residing. I never could figure out how he knew where I was at any particular time, especially the day he found me back again at the hospital in the emer-gency room. The time of conversation and prayer offered regular calm and comfort. How he found the time to care for his congregation in this manner is beyond me and was greatly appreciated throughout this time. These visits from the minister and others from our church also made it easier to return to Sunday services while still utilizing the wheelchair. Those first trips out were very stressful and the knowledge that there were others around who knew how to help me move around was very comforting.

Another scary part of so many injuries for me was the concern I would never be able to do the activities I previously did—and this turned out to be very true. Therefore, when friends brought over new activities for me to learn, it provided a different outlet that challenged my brain as well as provided a new interest. One friend brought over yarn, a crochet hook, and a pattern for a prayer shawl. During her visit she taught me to crochet and then returned to spend time crocheting together. This turned out to also be a fabulous form of occupational therapy for my broken wrist as, of course, this requires the use of both hands.

One friend knows that I am interested in art. She had attended a workshop on a form of line drawing and brought the supplies and shared the techniques with me. We spent a couple hours talking and drawing together. The next time she came we painted and decoupaged boxes. Then these boxes could be used to attractively store small items beside the bed. This created a positive memory every time I needed to access something from the box. Or created stress relief as I used the drawing technique to decorate a box of thank you notes. I lost these notes in the confusion of the basement cave-in so sadly they were never sent and shared as intended.

A friend of mine came from an hour away on several occasions and always offered to help with a required task. She helped me pack up kitchen items for hours even though I needed to take regular breaks and honestly, sitting in my wheelchair, I was more of an observer than a helper. She found a discounted cooking appliance which was beneficial to helping me cook healthy food in less time since standing in the kitchen was so difficult for me. She bought it and brought it so we could figure out how it worked together, recognizing that even setting up something as simple as a kitchen appliance was somewhat overwhelming and exhausting.

Over the months several friends came and stayed with my husband so that I could get out once or twice a month with friends. They would either hang out and watch sports together or help complete a couple items for me. A friend went into the basement and brought up our Christmas tree for us. I had asked him if he would get it out of the basement. I never expected him to actually set it up, which was an amazing surprise.

Our niece came and spent the time visiting and helping me go through our pantry. With the goal of a high protein diet there were several items that we would not be eating for some time and by then the items would expire. We sorted out what items could be taken to our food pantry at church and items that had actually already expired to be tossed. A friend from church picked up the food pantry items that were boxed and ready to go. I was happy to have the food used by others instead of being wasted.

Several times friends who came to keep either of us company would ask if they could help do a few things while they were at the house. Friends moved furniture, swept, cleaned, dusted, and changed lightbulbs. The list is endless as has been demonstrated in this book.

Caretaker Social Activities

If you are a walker or a fitness club person, offer to take a walk or encourage the caretaker to go to the gym with you. The caretaker may need encouragement to release stress or keep their body fit during this time. They may feel they do not have time for such activities. By doing something like a walk, you may be able to also help them release some stress and have some fun. In fact, think about it—we often spend a lot of time on the phone updating people. Suggest instead of a phone call that you join them for a walk around their block to get an update.

Another very generous offer is to stay with the injured or sick person so the caretaker can get out for a fun activity even when the person being cared for is in the hospital. It is hard for the caretaker to go out and have fun if they feel the person they love is sitting in a hospital looking at the walls or possibly not being taken care of properly. We want to guard our loved ones and sadly often need to do so. Until we are comfortable that the person is in a place where people will take good care of them, we spend every possible hour by their side checking in with doctors and nurses. We need to know someone will be there with them who will report any concern they might observe.

I asked friends to let me know when they thought they might be visiting with my husband. Even though I really would have enjoyed the chance to visit with them, I also knew that I could catch up on errands and other work when they were keeping my husband entertained and reducing his stress. It is tough because you are torn between wanting to be there when friends visit and you want your loved one to have company when you are not able to be there. If possible, guide the caretaker to take a deep breath and let them know that you can be there for both of them at the same time or at different times.

Caretaker Care

Ease their tasks.

We always think about helping with household and shopping daily activities when a person lives by themselves. I know for myself, in the past I have assumed when there were two people, the other person would be able to do such tasks when their spouse was unable to help. Everyone is different. It all depends on how the family lived prior to the event and how much time they had to prepare for the event.

The caretakers are incredibly stressed no matter how serious the issue is for their loved one. It is always harder to see a loved one suffering even if they have a minor cut on their finger. We want to take care of them and nurture them at the sake of our own well-being.

Some friends and family sent cards to both of us. A "thinking of you" card to the caretaker. A cat hanging from a tree limb with the saying, "hang in there." Something funny and light to help them understand we know this is hard for both people. Other items that can help are calming books on meditation, relaxation, comics, or content connected to the trials they are facing. Calming gifts such as lavender or a calming tea can be helpful. A trip to the spa or bubble bath works for some people. A notebook and fun pen for them helps them capture the activities of the day and any questions they may have along the way.

And this seems obvious but is regularly overlooked. Have you asked them how they are doing? Have they checked their own blood pressure and heart rate? Are they eating properly? Do they need company at the hospital or someone to stay with the injured or sick person so they can do other activities?

Words of encouragement or audio books might also be of help to both. A friend bought me lavender spray for my pillow to encourage sleeping. She also gave me a lovely expensive moisturizer which really cures dry hands. This was greatly appreciated because I was frequently washing my hands to be sanitary. A daily message book to read. The friend who gave me the message book would periodically ask me about a message that she found particularly inspirational. Snack bars to put in my bag when I went to the hospital. A supply of bottled beverages so that the caretaker can quickly grab one to take with them to the hospital protecting their hydration levels. Simply think about what helps you and go from there. Once again, if it comes from the heart, it is the right thing to do.

Not all caretakers are spouses and children. In many cases, there are other individuals who dedicate themselves to helping a friend or family member during a difficult time. If you are close to someone who is going out of their way to care for another, it can keep them energized or give them a boost to have someone do something particularly sweet for them—often something very simple like a light dinner, easy to eat snacks, a card, or flowers. Our niece took this concept to the next level. She wanted to do something nice for the man who was instrumental in saving my life the day the car pinned me against the post office inside wall. She found out some areas of interest for each family member and made a gift package for them including gift cards and a fleece blanket depicting our neighbor's favorite team. It was so sweet of her to take the time to not only be there to help and care for me after I was hit, she also recognized the considerable courage it took for this neighbor to stay by my side.

The Family Calendar

We are a society blessed with many opportunities for entertainment and family life. Some events are daily activities we often think about as repeated tasks: grocery shopping, clothing shopping, kid running, gardening, etc.—you understand—you do these things. Some events provide us with the joy of just being a part of the activity and the group involved: sports, bowling, family birthdays, holidays, etc.—those wonderful events that give us joy and contentment with life. And finally, there are those once in a lifetime events that happen which we look forward to for what seems like forever. They become the stories we tell our friends when we see them. Those events are not part of our normal activities so they give us that little extra boost. Activities such as a special vacation, an awards event, a graduation, a wedding, a special outing—events we often save for and sacrifice to make happen.

Then one day, something happens to totally change our work and fun activity calendar—an accident or an illness. The plan changes for the injured or ill person. And, the plan changes for the family and friends. This is an opportunity to recognize the person is not only dealing with loss based on their tragedy, they are dealing with the loss of that which provided them with excitement and joy.

Your involvement at this time can be the first step toward restoring joy to their life. First, because they are encouraged by the knowledge that you care. Then, as you are guided to keep those special events in the person's life, sometimes at a personal sacrifice.

Review the Calendar

Are you the person to sit down with the family and ask to review the calendar? Or the person to inquire if the holidays are covered? Is it Christmas or time for a birthday? Do you want to offer to buy a present for the person injured from the caretaker or a present for the caretaker from the person injured? It is often needed in both directions. The caretaker is so focused on only the essentials that taking time to shop for something special for the sick or injured person is simply outside the bounds of their energy. And clearly, the sick or injured person is probably not up to shopping or at least not on their own.

A dear friend asked my husband if he wanted her to shop for me for Christmas and for my birthday. Another friend bought my Christmas present for my husband and installed it—it was a soundbar for the TV since we were not able to go out at all. And this friend was very conscious about shopping for a good sale price since, as often happens with illness and injury, money was tight.

Is there a way to still give the person access to special events that they will now be missing? My husband had been co-chair of a local community showcase event for years. This event happened in the spring every other year because it completely consumes the time of many committee members. It is an event where local businesses, churches, and government entities can showcase what they have to offer our local citizens and community visitors. I wanted my husband to be able to honor his commitment to the team and continue his generosity to the community. In the past, in addition to being in charge of two days of entertainment planning and management, he also offered support to his co-chair who handled all of the event management. The spring that I was still unable to get around on my own, he still organized and managed the entertainment and others stepped up to offer assistance in other areas such as booth set-up. An activity that in the past I, too, would have done.

At the time, I was able to be at home by myself though still unable to come and go on my own. It would have meant me being home for the entire weekend by myself knowing I was missing all the fun. Friends traveled two hours, came to our house, loaded me into their car, and wheeled me around the community showcase even though it was not their community. They then took me out to eat and kept me company. This not only made the weekend enjoyable for me, it also gave my husband the comfort in knowing I was safe and well cared for during his absence.

Is there a way to share an event with the person if they are not able to attend? Think about a family wedding they will now miss but you will be attending—take video or extra photos you can share. Bring them their table favor, the program, or a piece of cake. Take photos of things like the decorations and table settings so you can share the day with them.

Was there a special outing they are no longer able to attend? Can you contact the organization to see if there is another date for the event? Are there ways for them to still feel connected to the event, such as a shirt that was going to be a part of their ticket? A DVD of the event or similar events?

If you stay with the sick or injured person, would it be possible for the caretaker to still go to a pre-planned event? Or maybe the children will miss out on activities if someone does not take them or encourage them.

Thanksgiving Dinner

We are often creatures of tradition which provides comfort and joy. Many times one person always hosts specific holidays and we all prepare the same or similar contributions each year. We never think about the travel that may be necessary to participate because it is part of the day's excitement and commitment to being with those we love.

Then, everything has changed: you are confined to bed, restricted from travel, financially not able to contribute, unable to host an event—the tradition is broken and you are sad and alone. Or are you? Does it need to be that way? Can you be thankful again? Even though things are different, can they still be wonderful?

Twice this has been a blessing in our lives during a time of crisis. Our newly married, amazing niece hosted Thanksgiving at her house because I could not travel any distance and she only lived five minutes away. It was our first attempt for me to leave the house at all. Our neighbor loaned us a travel ramp to get me into my niece's house. They set up the couch with pillows and bedding for me. We were told to bring nothing. And a team transported me from the car into the house careful to keep me safe. It was scary and it was wonderful! The love I felt inspired my healing and lessened the sadness I felt at not being able to travel to see my own mother. It was a very special day—a day of thanksgiving!

My brother-in-law teased as we planned the day that I was the queen since everyone was arranging their day and the house to accommodate my needs. So we chose to meet his humor with humor. My husband bought me a dollar crown which I then proceeded to wear when I arrived. We chanted, "The queen, the queen, she needs to reside on her throne." Tragedy is hard for everyone including those helping so it really lightens the situation if we can find a way to insert a smile or a laugh.

When my husband's mother was ill and could no longer host Thanksgiving, a cousin had us come share in their Thanksgiving even though the day was also her birthday. The entire family was in a transition time for the holidays. I have never forgotten that kindness—it is always a fond memory.

A Special Event

Sometimes, the blessings and love that fuel our recovery come from total strangers. A week after my husband had his stroke, we had tickets to a special night at the baseball ballpark—an event that my husband, who is a huge baseball fan, had planned for months. He had won the opportunity to be in a suite with one of his greatest baseball heroes, Mike Hargrove. Clearly, he was not going to be able to go. He asked his good friend, another big baseball fan, to take me since I was still struggling to get around and not up to driving any distance. Another friend stayed with my husband at the rehabilitation hospital. They watched the game together.

The first person I met in the suite was Sharon Hargrove, Mike's wife. I asked her to sign a bobble-head of her that my husband had gotten at an earlier game. She asked where he was and I explained briefly that he was in the hospital. From there the story unfolded in the most amazing way. She gave me the biggest hug and told me that as soon as he was better, they would invite us back up to the suite. She immediately wrote down her number for me to contact her and took my number. I was overjoyed that the event my husband was so sad to miss was going to now be part of his inspiration to recover quickly.

When my friend told Mike, he was as kind and concerned as Sharon about my husband's well-being. So much so that the next day, Sharon contacted me to say that she and Mike had talked and wanted to surprise my husband at the rehab hospital where he was recuperating. I was not to let the secret out of the bag. The look on my husband's face when they walked through the door was priceless. It was a wonderful visit. And the energy it provided for his healing carried him through as he shared the story with every friend who walked through the door to visit him. His energy positively changed as he focused on recounting such a positive event.

Baseball Baseball Baseball

My husband has had season tickets to the Cleveland Indians since the early 90's, the year before the team built a beautiful new stadium. It started with one twenty-game ticket and progressed to a full season shared with several friends. The tickets were in an inexpensive part of the stadium, we parked far away in the cheapest parking lots, and we always brought our own food into the ballpark. My husband loves baseball and I love sharing in the joy that going to the games provides him. I enjoy watching an exciting competition between teams, learning about the players, hanging out with friends, and enjoying the fresh air in good and bad weather. We were loyal to the team in good times and through the rough years when so many others moved on to other teams.

When my husband had his hip replacement, friends of ours took us to a game once he was allowed to leave home but was still not supposed to be without a walker. It took three of us to pull this off so that he could be dropped off right at the field. The ballpark has a service that allows those injured or needing handicap seats to do an exchange for the tickets. One friend stayed with my husband, I did the ticket exchange, and another friend parked the car. The entire night was a team effort in ensuring that a fun time was safely had by all.

Since my husband had his stroke, friends once again made it possible for him to attend his beloved Indians game as soon as he was able to be out in his wheelchair. I was not able to get him into and out of the car on my own due to my own injuries. Initially, friends from home came and loaded both of us up to go to a game, again enjoying the opportunity provided by the team organization to use the wheelchair accessible seats.

Then, as my husband became stronger, I would schedule with our neighbors who would help me get my husband and his wheelchair into our vehicle and we would meet friends from Cleveland at a more expensive nearby parking lot. We became friends over the years as we sat together game after game sharing the wins and losses that come with team sports. Though we wish we lived closer, this shows how close you can feel to friends whom you are only blessed to see 10 to 15 times throughout the summer baseball season. Our friend has experience caring for patients from her career and shared her knowledge with us; she encouraged us to come, ensuring with their help we would be able to keep both of us safe. They would meet us at the car and load my husband into his wheelchair. She would push him all the way to the stadium and wherever we needed to go inside. This ensured that my husband had someone to be with him while one of us would go get food or drink. Having a man as part of our group ensured he had someone who could help him to the restroom since our stadium has only three family bathrooms, none of which were generally near our seats. These friends, sacrificing their regular seats, would sit wherever we could get handicap seats in order to share the game with us as we had for over two decades. This gave us something to look forward to over the summer.

The Vacation Distraction

My passion in life was spending time with my family and friends first and traveling the world second. Quite frequently, I was able to combine the two. Most of our big trips were taken with either family or friends and many of our trips were to go visit family who live far away from us. The injuries I endured I thought were going to take this option away from me forever as traveling increases the risks of swelling, blood clots, and bites from creatures such as mosquitoes and bed bugs. Our dear friends with whom we frequently traveled were not inclined to agree with my assessment and wanted to give me a target to motivate my recovery. They booked a cabin for my husband and me on a cruise ship—they cruised frequently. They researched handicap amenities for, at the time, it was still not known if I would walk again. The land excursions would not be possible due to the risks and accessibility but there is so much to do on a ship that we would have been able to enjoy ourselves without ever departing. They formulated a strategy to safely get us to the departure site. Though this seemed scary, it gave me hope that I could return to the world that I most enjoyed.

This was before all of the other stuff then happened—the basement cave-in and my husband's stroke. Once these things happened, the trip was obviously cancelled and our friends went by themselves. They were wonderful and supportive throughout the process as we had to let go of the dream.

In fact, they worked hard once again to allow me to dream. They continued to encourage us after his stroke. They researched ways to free us from our home seclusion. Once my husband was able to ride in a car for a few hours, they invited us to stay at their house. The first visit, we hired another friend's daughter to go with us—she was in college to be an occupational therapist. She helped me get my husband safely into and out of the car. She devised the strategy to help him into their home. Our friends gave up their first floor master suite so we could have a comfy bed, a private bedroom, and an accessible bathroom. This felt like a luxury retreat since we have had to sleep in our living room since the stroke. They carried the luggage, set up the bedrail, and provided healthy food choices. Our friends took us out to a festival, wheeling my husband around to the different booths and leaving before any mosquitoes came out to keep my leg safe. Since then, they have invited us a few times as they know as well as I do how to keep my husband and me safe, entertained, and mobile. Instead of running around as we might have in the past, we stayed in and played games such as dominos. They always have things set up so that we can enjoy ourselves and get a much needed break from the day-to-day worries associated with our conditions.

Our family also did a similar kindness for us. They had invited us to their house a few times for a weekend giving us a mini vacation from our normal daily chores. Our pup was welcome to come with us and they took charge of getting her outside to do her personal business and to go for the walks she was not able to take anymore due to our issues. They shared the tasks required to assist my husband. We were blessed with yummy food and delightful company. The entire family learned how to assist my husband safely using his gait belt and kept him from falling more than once. My sister-in-law provided space where we could leave key essential items such as gloves and bleach wipes so we would have them ready for return visits.

Other friends have provided mini one-day or evening

vacations by loading us up in the car and driving us to a special location. They handled the planning and the orchestration to get us into and out of the fun locations.

It is amazing that, when one loses the opportunity to enjoy the things they have routinely done in the past, just how precious and important it is to find new ways to cherish life's moments. Our family and friends have always been our number one priority. Though I greatly miss being able to pack up and head out on a planned or spontaneous vacation, I feel blessed to have people who care so much that they created mini vacations for us to enjoy.

A Sentimental Kindness

I often feel I do not know a person well enough to come up with that perfect gift for home or hospital. I now believe, the knowledge that you care is what will touch the person's heart the most. Allow me to share a few of the kind treasures we received just to spark some ideas.

Cards and notes are the ageless gifts that are so inspirational and can be sent no matter the location of the sender or the recipient. My mother and a few friends kept the mailbox stocked with a continuous flow of cheery greetings. Welcome treasures to balance the constant flow of bills. I had cousins and friends who made cards with intricate designs that demonstrated an artistic talent I could only dream of attaining. I felt as if I should frame many of the handmade creations with their delicate images and multiple layers. E-cards are a fun option if the person still has access to their computer. Many e-cards are animated, providing additional entertainment. I loved the drawings from my nieces and nephews and would always encourage mailing those to a patient or dropping off a big stack of them. It is not only wonderful for the patient but also for the child to know they brought such cheer to someone going through a troubling time—a child's drawing is like a big hug. What fun to have some on the wall, door, or fridge when you are trying to slowly learn to walk again. And who can ever go wrong with balloons unless the person has an allergy to latex or has pets that could be scared or injured by the strings—there are sometimes additional factors to possibly consider.

Throughout this book there are examples of loving gifts made for us designed to support a physical need. My niece made me a lovely little fabric girl doll that reminds me of myself and continues to sit happily on my living room shelf. This doll supports an emotional need. A treasured hug from a sweet talented young lady. My explanation will not do justice to the detailed precise sewing that my niece demonstrates in her work. The tiny doll has brown yarn hair and a purple dress, one of my favorite colors as you can tell by the cover of this book. It sits next to an adorable paper box that she also made. The time she took to create such a lovely treasure always warms my heart. And, for me, it was a big hug during a time when it was impossible to hug anyone.

Several friends brought items to help distract me and my husband when each of us had to be in bed for so many, many months, both in and out of the hospital. Magazines that people knew we enjoyed before such as a dear friend who picked out sports magazines for my husband. Or collections of magazines we never knew even existed that we could scan through and widen our perspective. My neighbor and I always joke about reading brain candy—light enjoyable paperbacks that keep the mind engaged on a light-hearted, fun adventure so she and others fed my brain candy obsession. Other items include easy-to-handle and quick-to-complete puzzles especially for the hospital, adult or children's coloring books, and bright and colorful markers to use for writing or drawing.

With our physical therapy, some gifts that helped us use our hands in a fun way included brightly colored balls, easy to play games, or puzzles. We found playing cards to be another option. It is good to check with family members to determine that the gift is something within the current expectations of what the patient should be trying to do and not something that will remind them of what they are not able to do.

Flowers and plants bring considerable cheer and help to keep the air cleaner—ok, that would probably be too many plants. It feels cleaner though. When taking plants or flowers to a hospital or home, it is always best to take the water source also with you for hospitals are not equipped to offer vases or trays to keep water from pouring onto the surface. If you had a specific box that helped keep the vase upright during your drive to the hospital, ask the family if they would like the box to take the flowers home with the patient. We were always allowed flowers and plants at our locations yet I have heard some facilities do not allow them due to patient potential allergies—you may want to call ahead for the facility's policy.

I greatly enjoyed the many comforting treasures that traveled with me and with my husband from hospital room to hospital room in another facility thanks to the caring help of friends throughout each move. Friends provided me with stuffed animals which I hugged as I slept or which reminded me of our own furry child at home. Lovely inspirational gifts such as an angel or inspirational quote book were there to cheer up a stark hospital environment. My husband's friends gave him a signed baseball and actual art work that they attractively displayed in his room since he had such a long stay. My cousin brought me a mug that had a very inspirational positive energy, color, and message to encourage me daily as I drank my tea.

Friends and family knew how much we love holidays and holiday decorations so they brought small items to adorn the room and spread holiday cheer. I had so many decorations before the basement wall cave-in that I decorated two friends' houses one year after they had experienced the loss of a family member.

So my suggestion is let yourself be inspired and don't over think your approach. I did that myself recently. I wanted to do something for a friend who I have only recently gotten to know and do not feel I know well enough to know their taste or needs. I hesitated and hesitated until thankfully they recovered. I would much rather have done what was in my heart instead of doubting my approach.

A Holiday Vibe

In previous years we were known for our Holiday decorations both inside and out. In fact, one of our neighbors used to sneak a blue ribbon into our yard each year in appreciation for the job we did. To this day we only have suspicions as to which neighbor bestowed the award upon us. When seriously injured or sick, the holidays become a challenge, reducing the spontaneity and excitement. A drab interior due to the inability to carry decorations up from a basement or down from an attic. The dark yard that in prior years held a bright twinkling of light reinforces the sadness instead of inspiring holiday joy.

Knowing our love of Christmas, friends once again came to our rescue. Carrying up and setting up the Christmas tree. Helping to place decorations around the house to ensure a holiday vibe.

My husband's clients brought him a treasured retro tree that he had admired for years at their home for us to have. An amazing gift for it not only brought a smile to our faces for the current year but also brought back memories for my husband. Sometimes during difficult times it seems that celebrating the memories can also be supportive of living in a painful present—I am not sure how this works—it certainly did for me.

Another couple came every year to provide outside lighting and glow to the yard. They gave us lovely red outdoor lit bows to place on our new porch pillars and deer to adorn the flower bed. They then returned and packed up everything at an amazing speed with unprecedented organization. This year it may have frustrated a neighbor or two but I left a few of the lights on well into the spring because I was afraid of having unsafe footing in the dark now that we are able to leave our house again in the evenings—clearly we need some type of outside lighting. With both of our injuries it is dangerous to be walking around in the yard so having these friends decorate has been an amazing delight.

Our neighbor helped me each year set up our inflatable snow globe that we always enjoy, wishing everyone who passes a very Merry Christmas. He did not worry about whether it was muddy or cold—he simply volunteered to get it set up for our entertainment. He helped me set it up with new light bulbs inside. And a young teenager in our neighborhood came over and replaced all the light bulbs inside the snow globe when they burned out—this is surprisingly an extremely difficult challenge.

Before these things started happening to us, I decorated our house to the maximum. Little scenes and vignettes everywhere including an upside down Christmas tree which meant, prior to the basement cave-in that I had a complete Christmas shop in my basement. One year two of my friends lost family members and were struggling with enjoying the season as they had in the past. That year I pulled out extra trees and decorations and set them up at their houses ready to go to bring back some holiday cheer into their very difficult year.

Sometimes with additional medical equipment and supplies, the person does not have space for the holiday items of the past. Or they know that once they go up they must come down and that is a thought that is just too overwhelming. As always, communication is the best option. Some people want to have things the way they have been and other people just really want to simplify when things are difficult. And if their surfaces are filled with medical supplies, something that adorns the outside may be better or a pencil tree decorated in a corner might just do the trick. And as always, no matter what you do—if shared from the heart, it will all be wonderful.

Holidays Are So Important

It is important to be sensitive to which holidays a person or family celebrate. There are many holidays throughout the year which can be enjoyed in order to take the humdrum out of a long recovery.

A young couple on the street brought us a potted blooming clover plant for St. Patrick's Day. We surprisingly managed to keep it alive in order to be able to enjoy it annually on the front porch. My neighbor gave me a crimson clover and we still enjoy its festive color each year.

The same young couple brought over a basket of cookies for Valentine's Day. When she brought the cookies, she stayed for a visit while her husband watched the kids. We clearly were not getting out for the day so we very much enjoyed the special thoughtful surprise.

I have been making Christmas cookies with the same three women since I was in my late twenties. Every year we would either make cookies together or make cookies on our own and go to dinner to exchange our treats. The Christmas I was in bed, the group made extra cookies and brought over Chinese food. This gave my husband a chance to go out and spend time with his friends also. It was so wonderful to be able to continue to be a part of the tradition—a joyous event. We do not realize how missing out on one's normal activities and traditions becomes an additional loss.

Once we were able to make cookies again, our neighbor boy, who had been making cookies with us for at least the past six years, told us that he would once again like to come over and bake cookies with us. He was very patient helping my husband to be able to participate. He stayed with us the entire time even though it took twice as long as it did in prior years. Again, he really brightened our day and helped us to continue a treasured tradition. What a blessing to have a teenager with such compassion and kindness in our lives.

In order to have the traditional Christmas cookies that we had always associated with fun festivities, many people shared their time and their treasures with us. Cousins sent family traditional cookies. Friends helped make the cookies I needed to have for my annual holiday cookie exchange allowing me to continue to participate in the long-time tradition. My sisters and their families made a huge batch of time-consuming family favorites and delivered for our enjoyment and delight. And we got together with family for a fun day of cookie making, family stories, and food sharing—a tradition I hope will continue long into the future. Sorting out the new traditions is often a challenge in people's lives whether it is a tragedy or simply even a move—it is such a blessing when those around you recognize that life has changed for you and are so kind to share their holiday traditions with you.

Big Gestures Elicit Big Results

Holidays are so hard when you are trapped in your house and exhausted from healing and caring for others. Every gesture to share the excitement and festivities of a holiday are so special. These loving invitations help replace the feeling of loss that comes from missing one's prior traditions with the positive energy that comes from either a new tradition or a one-time generous acknowledgment.

I thought it was a very big deal that a group from our church choir took time out of their busy holiday schedule to come and sing Christmas songs at our front door. Think about it—Christmas is one of the busiest times of year for many and especially for a Christian church. The choir is practicing and performing frequently. Yet, this group of wonderful people bundled up to stand outside our front door on a cold Ohio December day to sing to us. I remember snuggling under a blanket in my wheelchair with the brisk winter air blowing on my face feeling all warm and loved by this group who took time away from their own families to share their gift of music. It truly helped to lift some of the sadness I had been feeling as we missed all of the holiday services. The choir came again the next winter when we were once again trapped in our home because of my husband's stroke. He has always loved music so this was a wonderful holiday gift.

One day we were outside on the sidewalk with a physical therapist helping my husband to stand and take some walker assisted steps. It was one of those days that when we walked out the door the sun was out. Suddenly, a cloud was overhead! It started to sprinkle and look ominously dark. The neighbor boy was on his way home from school and saw us. He quickly grabbed his umbrella and came racing over to provide some cover before the sky opened into a downpour. His father who was watching for him then did the same thing. Even though we were not far from home, at the very slow pace we could move, this young neighbor's quick thinking kept us from getting absolutely drenched which could have been dangerous for my leg.

Food, Oh Wonderful Food

Food is a very big subject and so very important in the life of a person in trouble. It is very critical for healing strength and energy for the one in need and those helping them face their challenge. For mothers of children, the concern is that their family still needs the healthy or nurturing care that has been their past norm. For those who need to learn how to cook for new diet requirements, they need the appropriate sustenance to give them time to focus on their current challenge and make the necessary grocery and cooking changes. For others, comfort foods may be the only items to entice their appetite.

First and foremost, never let anything I suggest stop you! Ideas such as placing food in disposable containers are simply that—ideas! If now is the time when you can help and you do not have a disposable container available, don't let the little details get in your way of an amazing caring connection.

If you are in the area and you think to drop off soup from a local restaurant, do so without worrying about all the questions or suggestions that I am capturing. The diverse consideration of the people who cared for me was amazing. I learned so many new alternatives and I am sure this will act as an inspiration for even more unique ideas. Just know that your kindness will be appreciated.

Even though I encourage finding out potential diet preferences and restrictions, I believe, as mentioned earlier, if you are inspired to provide a gift of food reflective of your specific talent, then there is a reason. An unexpected item may enhance the appetite for the entire family. The goal is for food to be available as needed whether researched or spontaneously provided.

The brains of the family members may have turned to mush—I do not mean this literally, of course. My concern is that the caretakers need to be focused on learning how to care for the injured or sick. I know I was emotionally drained from the stress and concern. It took two of us to care for my husband when he came home due to my own injuries. I rarely got any sleep. Therefore, even the task of remembering to thaw something for dinner or buy the right groceries was overwhelming. My husband had previously done most of the grocery shopping and healthy food preparation.

Whether you see yourself as a talented cook or not, your gift from the heart will help to sustain. A good friend told me she asked friends to make some peanut butter and jelly sandwiches for her children's lunches. Sometimes a loaf of good bread and some deli products are just what hits the spot.

Meal Delivery Planning

Is there someone coordinating food delivery? It is always nice to check. In my case there were several different people who offered to coordinate meal delivery which greatly helped us since I could not even get out of bed. Those individuals gathered information about our food preferences and dietary restrictions. They then suggested that everyone call us to determine the time of the food delivery and to inquire how many people would be at home that day. Sometimes we had a caretaker with us so it was nice that this person could be included in the meal. This also gave me the chance to ask people to join us for the meal.

Initially a group of women from our church coordinated daily meals. They informed everyone that the doctors wanted me on a low carbohydrate diet to promote wound healing. The coordinator asked us the following questions:

- Food preferences and restrictions
- Preferred dinner time (we were flexible)
- Number of people for dinner
- Visitors welcome or rest required

Due to the length of my bed stay, my hiking group

volunteered to take over the food delivery. This was very helpful and it was fun to once again see these friends. The group leader set up a calendar for food to be delivered every other day ensuring time to eat leftovers throughout.

As time continued, my neighbor knew of others who also wanted to provide food. She found an online website that allowed anyone to sign up indicating the day and dish they would provide. She then mailed friends, neighbors, and the church coordinator this website. She gave me the user name and password information so every day we simply checked the website to determine if a meal was to be delivered or if my husband needed to make other arrangements. When you are in a crisis, keeping track of information can be a challenge, so this really did simplify the entire process for everyone.

Food Communication

I say this with love and caring. Please do not interpret anything the person might say to be negative—remember that everyone involved is under stress. Why do I say this? What if the person meant to say, "I am now diabetic so I am avoiding processed sugars." Though without thinking because it is all new and stressful instead they say, "I can't believe she brought me an entire loaf of bread which I love but can no longer eat." And there you are baking fresh rolls to take over with your meal. You might be hurt by such a comment because you are a caring person and want to do what is best. Someone else might say, "I wish people would bring me something that I like to eat instead of trying to control my diet." And even diabetics eat carbohydrates so a fresh roll might be the perfect complement to go with an otherwise low carbohydrate meal.

Our neighbor will spontaneously check to see if we want dinner. She is a person who often takes food to other neighbors so she really appreciates when we let her know we already have dinner planned or do not like specific types of food. She doesn't like to see food go to waste. I let her know by saying, "No thank you, we do not eat fish" or "My husband would love some of that because it is a meal that I never cook."

We sometimes feel as if we cannot win in these situations. So the best we can do is to ask. The next best thing we can do is to simply act. Either action provides the person with the knowledge we love and care about them, which is the most important thing of all.

Determining the Meal Choice

If you want to check preferences, I suggest you contact the person, the family, or the meal planner. Indicate you really want to bring something they might enjoy so you would be interested to know if there are any food allergies, doctor's orders, or food preferences. As a person with a limited cooking repertoire, I suggest, if you have a couple of special dishes you are interested in preparing, that you are very clear and specific. You could say, "I was just at the grocery store. Would you like me to bring over some lasagna or meatloaf?"

My neighbor is the best at this. She lives on her own, is an amazing cook, and frequently tries new recipes. She will make a meal and call in the morning to see if we would like some for dinner. Yummmm!! And it is perfect! Usually the perfect amount for a meal. The recipes she tries are always more complicated than I typically prepare; therefore, providing us with a meal we otherwise would buy at a restaurant. Often more than enough for one meal. I love how she is so spontaneous and will let us know if she has made a special dessert or tried a new main dish. It is so sweet.

Please check regarding health or medication concerns since some people are medically restricted when it comes to deep green vegetables, nuts, seeds, sugars, dairy, gluten, or other food items. Or you can ask if they have had a lot of chicken, beef, pork, or fish delivered recently so you might try something of a different nature. The individuals who kindly coordinated our meal deliveries let those providing the meals know if several people were planning to bring the same dish within the same week. I greatly appreciated this, though when I don't have to cook it, I would enjoy the same dish for multiple days in a row.

If you enjoy cooking what I would call more adventurous foods, then by all means dig deeper—the opportunity try new recipes is wonderful especially when one is trying to learn to eat differently.

Remember, the person probably had food on hand when the emergency happened. Friends and relatives came and helped me clean out food that would spoil or that we could no longer eat due to our health concerns. I needed the space for medical supplies and not for foods we could no longer use. My niece rearranged items to ensure that what we needed most was closest to the work area since I had limited mobility. Some food was taken to the church for their food program because we would never be able to get to it before the expiration date. One friend cooked some of the food we liked so that we would have it to eat before it spoiled.

Now I have made meal giving sound regimented and cumbersome—again, don't let me discourage you. It is better to go with your heart on these things instead of being regulated by my research. The worst thing that can happen is that it only gets partially eaten.

Remember, the most healing part of bringing meals is letting the person know how much you care.

In summary, I must say that all research will tell you nutritious food is best for healing as well as reducing the impact of stress for the patient and the caretaker. Does that mean all comfort food is bad? Absolutely not, unless the person has a serious food allergy like a friend of mine who is allergic to peanuts or for someone with medication restrictions. If they have a special health concern, err on the healthy side or do a quick internet search for foods to absolutely avoid such as grapefruits which interferes certain medications. If you find great resources, share them. And then simply accept that we are not able to be an expert in all food areas and know that for the patient it will probably be a life-long learning process.

The Best Nutrition

If you are a person with healthy eating habits or knowledge about how nutrition impacts the condition facing a person in need, I would suggest checking in with the person or the person's family to see if they would like you to provide information or meet with them to share your knowledge.

We have a friend who doesn't eat any sugar. She would share her meals with us on many occasions and I greatly appreciated not only the night off from cooking but also the opportunity to learn a variety of healthier recipes. She would share some insights on how she has learned to make yummy options that do not contain processed sugars including a scrumptious rendition of a lasagna that uses vegetables as the noodles.

In my case, I was told by the doctor a high protein diet was critical for healing. I was very committed to following this advice due to the extensive nature of my wounds and the medical concern that they would not heal. I believe the advice was excellent since my wounds and bone did in fact heal at a faster rate than originally expected. In fact, my leg did not require additional bone graft surgery that had been anticipated.

Other people with medical issues such as lactose intolerance, heart disease, diverticulitis, or diabetes often need ideas on how to address eating for these conditions. They are stressed enough by learning about their medical conditions and going to appointments. If you have this expertise or personal experience, go ahead and share some hints and tips and, if those are well received, then you can offer to provide more. Always, of course, suggest that they confirm any dietary options with their nutritionist or doctor.

When my husband went into the hospital, a thoughtful friend prepared healthy favorites so I could provide him with food that would tempt his appetite. She included items that I never would have considered such as kale—she recommended I feed him half a cup a day because it is so nutritious.

Another friend suggested healthy snacks that again contain limited sugar. There was one snack that contained all natural peanut butter, oatmeal, and flaxseed rolled into little balls and frozen. What a quick and easy treat to keep one feeling full without reaching for something filled with sugars or bleached flour!

I found it so helpful when I was under such extreme stress to have samples of any suggested food options to determine if I liked the item before I went to the grocery store. To reduce the shopping time I would buy those foods which were quick and easy to make even when I knew they were not the best food choices. Once friends gave me samples and recipes, it became easier to buy the healthier options.

If you are aware of good books, apps, nutrition classes, nutritionists that work privately, local hospital or health club nutrition programs, restaurants, or other healthy venues—these can help the person transition to a healthier lifestyle. Our Sunday school gave us a gift certificate to a business that specialized in home healthy cooking.

A friend gave me a diabetic cookbook that a member of her family had found to be extremely helpful. Once I was able to start cooking again I loved it. I asked my husband to go through and mark recipes he wanted me to try. We slowly increased the number of recipes that we enjoyed. This cookbook provides a new meal suggestion for every day of the year without any repetition. The fact that she knew someone who had used the cookbook with great success and then shared the book with us was a tremendous help.

Caretaker Eating

When a person has a loved one in the hospital, especially for an extended stay, I suggest helping to ensure the caretakers are eating properly—or at least eating. They will often be more likely to pick up fast food or eat from the hospital vending machine if there is one handy. The worst thing is they may not eat or drink because they don't want to be out of the room should one of the medical team choose that time to come for a consultation. The family is more likely to take the time to eat healthy food when provided. We all know that making food requires shopping, preparing, and sitting down to eat—when they are feeling as if they don't have time to even sit down, they will not prepare a meal for themselves.

For me, knowing that people were providing my husband with food when I was in the hospital was not only a benefit to him—it gave me comfort. When a person is dividing their time between the hospital and work, meals become the last priority. This is where I might suggest taking the opportunity to just be a "little pushy." I use those terms lightly. When in the midst of a crisis, I feel we try to say that we are fine and believe we should be able to fend for ourselves. I know both my husband and I said that we would be fine. Thank goodness for those friends who just did not listen. In reality it is not that anyone wants to waste food, yet it is the worst thing that would happen by surprising someone with an extra plate of what you are eating. Without their help, I might have eaten my favorite ice cream for breakfast, lunch, and dinner more than once. I never knew that a strict ice cream diet could result in weight loss but it did. Please don't take this as dieting advice. But what I lacked without the help of others were veggies, fruit, water to go, and healthy beverages.

When I came home from visiting my husband in the hospital, I was exhausted and sometimes didn't even bother to eat. Something quick and simple to heat up can be a great treat. Or, I thought it was so sweet when our neighbor across the street saw me come home and asked if I liked pizza. They had just had a pizza delivered. She brought over a couple pieces and a can of soda (pop). She stayed to get an update and see how I was doing while I ate my pizza. For me it was wonderful to sit for half an hour on the front porch enjoying her company while I munched.

On my birthday, friends picked up food and brought it to the hospital to have a birthday party for me that my husband could then attend. There was a common room we were allowed to use so we all sat around the table and had a birthday celebration. Just because you are eating in the hospital does not mean that the food needs to be made by the hospital. Though if you are eating anything unusual, it could be good to let the hospital know if the patient has shared in the meal so they can identify any concerns that food may introduce to the patient's numbers that day.

I am going to sneak in one more suggestion. Pack a healthy snack cooler for the family member spending so much time in the hospital. When our aunt went to the emergency room and we were staying with our cousin, I quickly grabbed a couple of bananas, two bottles of water, and crackers with cheese for them to take to the hospital. We spend hours waiting for doctors and emergency personnel afraid to leave the waiting area for that is when the doctor will come by with news—send them with healthy alternatives to the vending machine even if there is a vending machine handy.

Or when you head to the hospital to visit, hand them what I call a "Go-bag." This is a bag containing a few non-perishable healthy and non-healthy snacks. Either homemade treats or individual little snack items in an easy to carry bag. The drawstring bags available in dollar stores work great. In my case, when I had some granola bars, protein bars, tiny snack candy bites, pretzels, nuts, and a bottle of water, I could focus on my husband at the hospital.

A Delivered Meal

I was so incredibly amazed by the variety and regularity of the food that arrived at our house. Everything from soup prepared by a local restaurant to complex meals with multiple sides prepared in the home of friends and strangers. With everything that happened we were not able to thank everyone with a card so I hope everyone, through our profound verbal thanks, understood how they in fact kept us strong not only through the sustenance provided but also through the energy such kindness generated toward our determination. I had started to write thank you notes when I was still in bed but no longer required 24 hour care—

then the basement wall caved in and I still am not sure where they ended up during the chaos. My friends told me that everyone knew how much I appreciated them and that focusing on moving forward was critical for us. I definitely want everyone who brought us food to know how much we greatly enjoyed both the nourishment and the visit.

We know that several people cooked a meal just for us with all the side dishes anyone could imagine—fruit, meat, potato, salad, and bread. One friend always brought cut up fruit when she delivered a meal. Other people would make an extra serving of the meal they were having for dinner that evening. One friend froze a couple servings as they ate dinner throughout the week and then delivered two or three frozen entrées she had prepared. We loved the variety.

We learned different options for packaging meals to deliver that we found to be very creative. If you use containers you would like returned, we found it very helpful if they were marked in some way or came with a note indicating what needed returned and had a phone number handily included. Sadly, when under stress, the caretaker can be challenged to remember things they previously remembered and completed with ease. Other options that worked well included take-out containers repurposed, sturdy disposable plates with aluminum foil on top, and the always functional storage bags. One friend would bring two plates of food already portioned out on microwaveable disposable plates covered in aluminum foil—this made preparation and clean-up extremely fast. She included a salad in a cool whip container on the side.

One friend impressed us with her organization skills. She arrived with her food in freezer storage bags. She used a felt tip marker to identify the food and the preparation date on the bag. She asked if we wanted it for dinner that night. If we were not going to eat it that night, she would place it in the freezer or fridge. She then left the pen and some extra baggies for other meals that would be delivered by others. We found when we were overwhelmed, it was often hard to remember what meal we ate what day and know if the leftovers were still safe to eat. We learned it was helpful to know when the food was prepared, not delivered. This approach gave us better tools to keep track of our food by freezing or eating it before it spoiled.

Our friends would give us a call to find out when they could drop off food. You can drop and run. Or stay and chat depending on how you gauge their energy. When we were in the hospital, it was hard to catch us at home. It was great that we had a close friend who spent a lot of time helping at the house who could be there for delivered food. Another friend brought over a cooler and put it on our porch for people to use.

The lesson I learned the most from this is it is important to go with your heart and not hesitate because you are not sure what people will eat. We learned that we liked foods we never knew we liked and we learned that food from friends who care is a big hug when you are in chaos.

Join in the Meal

Determining if you should join in the meal can be a challenging part of the equation. I wanted people to join us for dinner! Our prior behavior was to frequently eat out and socialize. After coming home from the hospital, when people stayed for dinner it gave me the feeling of going out with friends. Note that other people really like to be left alone when not feeling their best. Communication, therefore, is challenging because people really don't want to hurt others. So, the best you can do is to ask and it is the person's responsibility to make their wishes known. And the food preparer's responsibility to not take it personally because the person's wishes may vary day by day as they have good and bad days.

We were always happy to provide the dishes and everything else that supports dining together. It was also fun when people came who treated the event like a picnic. One friend came with pretty plates, coordinated napkins, plastic glasses, and even their own personal silverware. She set out a lovely table and then scooped it all back into her picnic basket and there was not a thing to do when she left. Bringing the dishes is clearly above and beyond and something I wouldn't have thought about doing.

And though we were happy to do the clean up after not having to prepare the food, it was so sweet when others either packaged up the leftovers in containers that they brought or loaded the dishwasher before they left. It is possible some people are tired once the meal is completed and are ready to rest. Those individuals may prefer to leave the non-critical cleaning until the next morning.

Therefore, I am not able to tell you who needs rest and who prefers the wonderful distraction and interaction with friends. This goes back to our appreciation that people are energized differently. The best I can suggest is that you first consider how they lived their life before. Did they seem to prefer quiet time? Were they always around people? Use that as your first guide. Did they eat out or in? And then, I prefer the direct approach. Ask and then watch for signs of exhaustion.

I had a friend who dropped off dinner and started to race out the door. I looked in surprise and asked if she had time to stop and chat. She looked at me in surprise and said, "You want me to stay? I have always felt like I was exhausting the patient if I stayed. I figured you would prefer to rest."

I, as the patient and the caretaker, loved the interaction before, during, and after the meal. We were trapped for almost three years without being able to leave our house unless we had an entourage of friends to help us. So, we loved the company. When my husband was ready to sleep after dinner, I enjoyed the continued company as we cleaned up after the meal. This is all very complicated isn't it? Again, ask gentle open-ended questions and observe the responses with both eyes and ears.

↜ Ice Cream and Fun Treats

In our world we called this comfort food and motivation food. We strove to eat healthy for healing consistently. And we treated ourselves, thanks to the kindness of others, when we really needed a pick-me-up or when we hit all of our goals for the day. We were also able to share the treats provided with others who came to help us throughout the day as we would have done in our previous uninjured life.

A friend of ours who has ice cream connections and knows how much we enjoy going to our favorite ice cream shop made sure we were never out of stock of our favorite flavors.

Another friend made sure we were never out of stock of our favorite chocolate chip cookies. Early on she packaged them in smaller bags and placed them in the freezer. Later after we were doing physical therapy she wrote a friendly note suggesting we use them as a reward for completing daily therapy activities. How inspiring is that?!!

A dear friend provided cut up fruit knowing how much we love fresh fruit as a treat. A neighbor delivered a fruit basket.

Friends and neighbors provided holiday cookies and candies to ensure we were participating in the holiday festivities when I was not able to bake the cookies that I usually made. I was able to freeze some to enjoy later. The kindness given to us not only provided us with love but also allowed us to ensure those who spent hours at our house helping were treated with the kindness we previously shared.

We have friends who still provide us with our favorite treats knowing that staying on track and motivated with all the doctors appointments, medical research chores, physical therapy, and occupational therapy required is exhausting. An occasional special treat with a glass of milk is just the medicine we need.

Heavy Hydration Groceries

Grocery and supply shopping was one of the hardest things for me to complete when my husband went into the hospital. With my injuries, he was doing all of the shopping and basically all of anything physical. I was barely walking and still using a cane. My left wrist was still too weak to carry anything except for the lightest items. Having plenty of beverages on hand was critical to my staying hydrated as was required for my well being. A variety of healthy beverages provided by friends was especially helpful.

Staying hydrated can be one of the hardest things to do when you are trying to handle life with a loved one in need. On top of your normal activities, you now have the task of being someone else's support and care team leader. In my case, I was in the midst of researching my own care options and attending my own physical therapy appointments. I had a house that was still under construction from the basement cave-in. My leg needed special care and to be elevated as much as possible.

Individual bottled water or other beverages were very helpful for carrying to and from the hospital. Yet clearly I could not carry a case of water, and buying water by the individual bottle is cost prohibitive on a frequent basis. A good friend periodically brought over a case of water from a big box store so that I could easily grab one bottle at a time and be ready to go. A neighbor asked if I needed anything and I asked for a bottle of a sport drink because they help me when I have a headache. They showed up with several large bottles.

Hydration was critical for my healing but water was getting very tiresome as my only source of beverage. Another friend told us about beverage flavorings that could easily be added to our regular bottles of water in order to encourage us to drink more—I never knew these things existed and clearly they are a lot lighter to carry home from the store. We found it saved us money and space when combined with filtered tap water.

Another friend gave me a filter bottle that would allow

me to carry this light weight reusable container everywhere and then use the tap water no matter where I went. This again was very helpful since of course I needed to carry other things to and from the rehabilitation hospital for my husband. I then bought one from her for my husband to use at the hospital as the hospital water had a weird flavor and filtered water seemed like a healthier option.

A friend brought milk weekly, making sure the date was far enough out for the milk to last until her next shopping trip. Knowing that I continued to have trouble carrying heavy items even after my husband came home, she continued to bring the milk for a very very long time—over a year. She knew how a large warm cup of milk at bedtime seemed to help me relax and supplemented my diet on days with limited food. And I looked forward to spending some time with her when she made her delivery. My husband even commented, if we did not see her for a longer period of time, how much he missed her visits. This friend had a key to our house as a back-up during this time so one day we came home from a doctor's appointment and there was milk tucked into the fridge just as we ran out. It made me smile!

Groceries Predicate Meals

If you happen to live near the person, just call when you are headed to the grocery store and ask if they would like you to pick up something. As mentioned before, walking and carrying was and is very difficult for me since my injuries. So having food at home and healthy food to entice my husband's appetite at the hospital was an overwhelming task.

Many friends and neighbors would call when they headed to the store to ensure whether we needed any items added to their list. I would at first ask for only those items that were absolutely critical or heavy, thinking I would be able to make it to the store for other items. Believe your friends and neighbors that they want to help and accept the help with the love and kindness it is intended. They are not able to read your mind and, even if they know you well, they probably don't have a clear understanding of your food preferences or needs.

An individual or a group can choose to provide weekly grocery shopping. Ask the injured person to provide a clear list of needed items specifying quantity and brand preferences. The person could even email or text the grocery list on a specific day. A person should specify if they care about brand, color, flavor, etc. Or, if any flavor or size is fine. A specific notebook could be provided for the grocery list. And if you want to offer to grocery shop for one or two weeks, it never hurts to specify the intended duration. You can always add on more time if you feel it is necessary.

Right after my husband went into the hospital, a friend asked me for my grocery list. I asked for supplies to make a pasta salad heavy on the veggies with a quinoa pasta to entice my husband's appetite while controlling the amount of carbohydrates. I planned to make it one evening in order that we both might eat it for several days. I got home that evening exhausted expecting to need to make food and she arrived with the entire load of groceries and a big disposable container of the pasta salad already prepared. At a time of such stress it was like being given a two hour spa treatment. I just did a head shake—I would have been up for a couple hours to make the pasta salad. Again, with my injuries everything took so much time. Instead of cooking into the wee hours, I got to go to bed early that night. I supplemented the hospital food that was not enticing my husband to eat—he enjoyed it very much.

Many people will feel more comfortable asking others to shop for them if they know that the shopper will let them pay for their items. If you, the shopper, want to pay, let the person know that the first trip is on you and then they can pay for future trips. Or give them a gift card for a specified amount to the grocery store you use. Then they can pay for any additional cost above the gift card. Have the items rung up on a separate sales slip so an accurate price is automatically recorded.

Just recognize that communication is challenging, but essential to avoid confusion and uncomfortable situations. You may even say if you are uncomfortable buying certain products because you are unfamiliar with how to determine the best quality—I would never know how to determine a fresh fish item. I know my friends found it helpful when I let them know if I had any parameters such as we always drink two percent milk.

One approach might sound like this, "I would be happy to buy your groceries for you when I go each week. I will have to let you know what day I am going because it varies. I can have your groceries rung up separately and simply leave the receipt with the groceries. I have to admit that I rarely buy meat so I am not sure how to determine the best options. Please help me by writing down a detailed list. I know I will be able to do this through the end of the month and then our schedule may get a little crazy so I won't be able to shop after that."

Why do I suggest that if the person is able, that you allow them to pay for their items? Because my concern is that they will not allow you to do their shopping for them regularly if they feel they are adding to your financial expense. And why do I suggest you be very specific about things like duration or grocery shopping schedules? Because you don't want someone who is counting on you to shop and then realizing that you are no longer available. Our sweet milk shopper knew how hard it was for me to carry items and bought our milk for a very long time. Once I figured out how to carry it with two hands, I told her I would be able to buy it myself. We did miss seeing her every week once she stopped her delivery process.

And if the person is not going to be at home, ask them

to leave a cooler for the food. This would allow you both not to be restricted by the person's unpredictable schedule. Ice packs are very inexpensive, so you could keep a couple rotating for cooling and deliver the ice pack with the groceries.

ঌ Stocking Up

If food and cooking are not your thing as it was not for me before this happened, there are other food-related activities that we found to be very helpful. Our friend belonged to a bulk purchasing chain store. She had a list of items we used regularly and would check in to see if I needed any of them picked up when she went. She would watch for coupons and buy these items when they would go on special. With injuries and medical issues, a person may find a need for more sanitary cleaning supplies. We buy key items in bulk such as medical gloves, cleaning gloves, paper products, bleach wipes, hand wipes, and nuts.

My aunt shared the following idea with me. When a person has experienced a loss, an illness, or any event where numerous people may be in and out of the home, receiving the gift of paper products is an unexpected treasure. It is so much easier to have your toilet paper delivered than to have to make trips to the local store to stock up on paper products. A friend told me how she uses this idea to welcome new neighbors. Though not a trauma in the traditional sense, have you ever moved? What a great idea to welcome a new neighbor with not having to wash dishes before they are even unpacked!

I had forgotten this idea but will bring it back in my own repertoire of ideas. When my sister was going through a particularly stressful time, I took a box and wrapped it in a lovely floral paper. These days it is possible to find lovely boxes already made or to use contact paper to cover a box. The box was the perfect size to fit on or under the table and held all the paper products necessary to eat a meal. This way she could set and clear the table quickly as I also included trash bags.

Or offer to take them with you when you go shopping to stock up and reduce the difficult errands. We eat a lot of nuts and our friend would take me with her to stock up on our favorite healthy snack packs. This also reduced our expenses and ensured when heading out to different appointments that we never went hungry.

Grocery Store Alternatives

If you are aware of food services in the area, this would be very helpful for a home-bound person. We had friends offer many such suggestions which proved enormously helpful for ongoing support. For example, there was a bulk food fundraiser that was run by our local school system. One friend bought from them each month so she would add on anything we wanted and simply tell us what we owed. She would place the order, pick up the food with her order, and drop everything off. The foods that she brought lasted the entire month, such as staples like frozen pre-cooked chicken and broccoli. Many times she supplied the food or added an item at her own expense thinking it would be a great healthy quick meal idea. Or she would try a new item and split the order with us so we both could try it out. We not only appreciated the incredible kindness, we also enjoyed the chance to catch up with her whenever she delivered the groceries.

Another friend told us about a grocery store drive-up window. I never tried it because of the distance to that store. I never knew there was such a thing and, had I known about it when I was still using the cane, I definitely would have used the service. I did initially ask for help in taking my groceries out to my car and found everyone to be incredibly nice about doing so.

The online food delivery programs are also a possibility. Though they reduce the grocery shopping steps, someone would still need to stand and prepare the food. A recommendation would definitely be helpful because when I researched them I became overwhelmed by the options. It helped me when a friend shared the information on the one she used.

Freshly Grown Items

If you are growing things or picking from a local farm,

it is wonderful to ask if you can pick up any items for the person. In this case, you may want to check in advance as to the person's budget because, depending on the farm market and season, prices can vary.

A friend brought us luscious strawberries fresh from the field several years in a row. She goes to the farm every year to pick and would contact us to make sure we were going to be able to use them so they would not spoil. We would dive into those berries the moment they were delivered because we really missed our annual berry-picking expeditions.

A neighbor gave us a big bag of just picked tomatoes. In the past we were always the tomato providers. Our garden at the side of the house was often filled with numerous tomato varieties which I enjoyed sharing with our neighbors. Tomatoes have always been a summer staple in my diet having grown up on a farm.

A third friend delivered a fresh box of blueberries for us to eat and freeze—yum. I mean a huge box! I can't recall how many pounds. She orders them every year from a local farm and they are incredibly fresh. She gave us the box of berries and the information for us to continue ordering them each year.

My mother's friend grows the most amazing garden. He would send us baskets of fresh food to eat at no charge. There would always be tomatoes, squash, string beans, and garlic throughout the season. In the fall he provided veggies that lasted for months including monster sweet potatoes. This past year there was one in the shape of a swan.

Another friend let me know about a farmer who delivers if you order more than $25. He also provided breads, soups, and granola. This allowed me to order fresh vegetables that we would have previously purchased at a farmers market, an adventure that is no longer something that we are able to enjoy.

Annually, we used to buy a case of either oranges or peaches from a truck that delivers from the southern states. We were not able to go so a friend agreed to meet the truck for us when it was orange and peach time. We have to watch how much fruit we eat. A fresh peach or orange provides incredible nutrition and keeps one away from the highly processed sweets.

We are no longer able to have a traditional garden. Instead we are trying to use pots on the porch to grow some fresh-picked veggies on a much smaller scale. Friends ordered pots online for us to try to improve our success in this endeavor and to be able to grow more options within a very small space.

A Monetary Gift

Several friends provided us with gift cards to grocery stores, restaurants, and food preparation companies. This was very helpful in two ways. First, it relieved the financial pressure and psychologically allowed one to spend what seems to be extra money on good quality, healthier cuts of meat and veggies. Second, the gift card may be handed to another individual going to a grocery store in order for them to buy groceries on your behalf. Or the cards may be used to call ahead to a restaurant and take home fully prepared meals.

Some groups from church gave us cards with gifts of cash for us to use however we needed. Again, financially, this was incredibly helpful! And, it provided us with some cash on hand. We found it helped to have a variety of denominations handy so we could immediately reimburse funds.

Dining Out

Prior to the injuries we enjoyed eating out as couple-time and friendship-time. Once the injuries happened, the two of us could not go to a restaurant on our own. Friends and family made it possible for us to go by pushing my husband in his wheelchair or, more recently, spotting him with his walker.

I know that prior to this I probably would have hesitated to approach someone in a walker or wheelchair to offer assistance. Thank goodness others are more open. A friend who helped my husband with his physical therapy was the first to take us out as a reward for the hard work. When we got to the restaurant, the waitress was so very, very sweet. She moved tables and made it possible for us all to have the most delightful outing that was possible. Guess what? We went back and it continues to be one of our favorite places. We usually end up with the same waitress and she always remembers that we drink water and what we usually order. She stores the walker and returns it when we are ready to leave.

Other friends and family have also taken us out to eat. They handled getting the wheelchair in and out of the vehicles, maneuvered my husband through the restaurant or event location, and have assisted my husband with cutting his food. When my husband transitioned to being able to use a power chair, we discovered that your movement is still often very limited in many facilities making it impossible to use the chair. Starting with the fact that parking lots often do not have the space for a van with a ramp. You will see when you go out for the night, now that you have read this book, that most restaurants and party facilities do not have space for power chair seating. To go out to a new place, we have always taken people with us because you need multiple people to park the car, ensure usable access, ensure bathroom access, and assist with potential seating. And don't get me started on the new high top trend that neither of us are able to utilize.

When I figured out my husband could use a walker for short distances, I could in familiar situations take my husband to appointments and restaurants without needing an entire crew. I have been so very thankful for total strangers many times. People who assisted with doors including restaurant hostesses and servers. A group of men who came out of nowhere to help one time when my friend and I were spotting my husband using his walker and he started to fall. The two of us were struggling as we kept him from going down, but were unable to help him regain his stable footing. These men came to our rescue and were able to carefully lift him using the gait belt, a safety strap around his body. That was so scary and I cannot imagine the outcome without such kindness of strangers.

For any situations that required a regular wheelchair, we needed a team to help, because my injuries prevented me from assisting him.

Returning to Work is Scary

Imagine this scenario as if you are in another person's shoes. You have not been to work for months. You are the same person you were though you now look different! Or, maybe you don't look different but now everyone knows intimate details about you and what has happened in your life. Though you believe they care, you cannot help feeling vulnerable. Will they see you the same as you were before? Can they look past what you have been through and see you as the strong employee or business associate that you still are?

For many, the trauma is not visible. Is this good or is this a challenge? What if you need to have a moment during the day to stretch your injuries, to eat a healthy snack, or just to catch your breath? Yes, in the past you could go from meeting to meeting and not need to stop. Now you need to take care of yourself as well as your work. Both are possible—just not your prior norm. For many the trauma has left a physical change as in our case. Are people able to look past those changes and recognize that you are still the same person?

For me, I spent nine months primarily in bed. Just as I was starting to walk, our basement wall caved in. A month later my husband had a stroke. I was constantly exhausted. I had limited strength and mobility. I was still using a cane to get around. I looked different than before—my hair was super long, scraggly, and half gray. I could no longer wear dresses or business suits. My leg injuries resulted in most of my pants and none of my shoes being wearable.

I am an independent consultant who was used to working odd hours per the client's needs, heading out to evening meetings in full business attire. And though on one level I wanted to believe that work knowledge is all that I needed, I am well aware that every business coach will tell you first impressions are critical.

My work identity had become uprooted. Several people encouraged me to get back into the work world. For my husband and myself, those people were not the doctors. One of my doctors said, while encouraging us to seek disability options, that my husband and I would probably never work again. We are in our early 50's and now saddled with a myriad of medical and home needs. We need to work again! We have to work again for financial necessity and self-satisfaction. Yes, we were on target for retirement in 10 years. Now, that money has been used to pay medical and rehabilitation expenses. More importantly, to provide continued rehabilitation. To enjoy contact with the outside world. If we are not working, we would be at home staring at each other and the same four walls 24 hours a day 7 days a week. Though we are each other's support, we treasure the time we can spend with others.

Early on while I was still mostly in bed or caring constantly for my husband, a vendor of mine gave me small projects to complete. These projects were items I could do from home with my leg elevated. This gave me the confidence and encouragement to keep moving forward. Much of the work I ended up doing in the middle of the night while my husband was sleeping. On the one hand I was exhausted by the process and they were very kind and understanding—more than I ever could have expected. On the other hand, they showed me I was still respected and my work was of value. I know this does not work for everyone. Yet, there are often projects that need to be done by employers or by non-profits that could be done from a person's home. It is not always about paid work, it is often about staying connected and feeling needed. So, if the person belonged to a community organization that could use some assistance with phone calls, emails, or mailing, would it be a good or bad thing to see if they have any energy or time to help? No pressure because medical challenges can take up almost every minute. Sometimes it really helps to know that those with whom you worked before still would like to have you there once again.

ঌ She Reinvents Herself

I want to thank everyone who encouraged me to move forward and reinvent myself and how I approach my career. Prior to my injuries, I would hop on a plane and go to any location within the United States. Work whatever hours the client needed in order to meet a deadline. I am no longer able to commit 60 or more hours in any one week. And, I can no longer travel as I did before. I still would love to do my consulting. I think I could easily translate my manufacturing and retail experience to the medical world. Now having seen the inner workings of the medical world, I have an incredible amount to offer in the areas of employee motivation, employee contribution to organization enhancement, patient customer service, organization funding achievement, and organization recognition.

Until that day comes, I am thankful that a group of women, my inspiration team, encouraged me to write a book about the stories of kind deeds that everyone had done to help us. Most of it was written as I was lying in bed. Before going to press, I have been working to add many of the additional wonderful feats of others to support our development. These same women then encouraged me to speak to groups regarding the ways that others may be an inspiration to those that they know. I have spoken on many topics before; I have never spoken on a topic about myself and this caused me considerable angst. I am a consultant and coach—behind the scenes helping to empower others to achieve the best results for themselves and their businesses. This is a guide designed to reduce the uncertainty that exists for many of us who are not comfortable knowing what help to offer and who, when injured, are not comfortable asking for help. My prior employment required that I be certified in presentation skills. My inspiration team encouraged me to attend a seminar on building a speaking business. People jumped in to stay with my husband in order that I might attend the eight sessions of the program. Friends assisted me in getting to and from the sessions.

I walked into the first program very uncomfortable because I was no longer in my element. As a result of my injuries, I am no longer able to color my hair. My hair was past my waist in length and at the time half gray and half brown—I mean bottom part brown and top part gray. My leg was bandaged and my feet were clad in men's heavy duty tennis shoes. My right shoe is three full sizes bigger than my left shoe in order to accommodate the extensive compression bandages. My clothing was big and baggie to again accommodate the bandaging. My entire body weakened by a lengthy bed stay slouched when I stood and sat. I pulled into the parking lot, lifted my head high, straightened my back and shoulders, and headed into the meeting early, introducing myself to the instructors and my new course-mates. I almost wanted to slide under my desk when one of the women after my introduction said in an attempt to be funny, "I wondered why you were wearing such ugly shoes." Though she meant to be kidding, it was uncomfortable. During the class sessions that followed, I greatly appreciated the instructtors who made it a safe place to get back into my career and expand my career into a new direction.

Friends and complete strangers continued to help me move forward because it is so hard to stay focused on your career when your energy is so consumed by the care of a loved one and your own injuries. It is hard to maintain your energy when your sleep is constantly interrupted again due to the basic care needs placed upon you each day. These friends and family encouraged me to move forward on the book. They read what I wrote, offering feedback and input. My sister read every last word multiple times, editing each version as I kept adding more and more content—I would constantly remember one more kindness bestowed upon us which I thought might inspire someone else.

As I moved forward with the book development, I learned many things the hard way—trial and error. Thankfully, others whom I had never met before shared the knowledge they gained in publishing their own books. These individuals provided information on how to simplify the writing and publishing process which will serve me well in my future endeavors, allowing me to get content out the door faster than the years it has taken to produce this book.

Though I still struggle to balance the home health challenges and the advancement of my career, I know that I have the support of so many encouraging people to help me along the journey.

He Is Able to Work Again

The reality for my husband was that he needed to do hours and hours of physical and occupational therapies in order to regain any use of his right arm/hand and leg/foot. This in itself was exhausting mentally and physically.

Initially, his office co-workers and clients were extremely patient. His co-workers ensured his clients received the best possible care during his absence contacting him for direction as was needed. His assistant aided me in knowing any licensure testing that needed to be completed to ensure everything stayed up to date and we worked together to determine the best options for completion. His business associates managed the purchasing and set-up of a laptop for him to use at home ensuring the appropriate software and security were in place. This kept him in contact with his clients and able to ensure they were appropriately advised while he was still unable to leave the home environment.

As his energy increased, his friends came to the rescue—literally. Without them, my husband never would have been able to return to work. I was not able to help him in and out of the house or office. I was not and am still not strong enough to lift a wheelchair or push anyone in a wheelchair. A group of friends started taking him into work a few hours a week building up over time. At first, he would go into work in sweat pants and t-shirts. One day his transportation friend looked at him and said in a very kind way, "wouldn't you feel better at work wearing business clothing?" This was not something I had pushed because at the time I was still helping him with all aspects of dressing and again this was not easy with my own injuries. I saw the benefits as I myself was starting to take more care in my own appearance. If clients were going to come into the office, they needed to see him physically as well as mentally focused. As time went on, thanks to excellent occupational therapy, he was able to do more of his own preparation and go into work more frequently. He built up his in-office time to three short days a week and one friend who recently retired took charge of ensuring he had a ride to work on Monday, Wednesday, and Friday. We scheduled his physical and occupational therapy around his work hours and more heavily on his off days.

When my husband finished the left gas pedal driving training and test, he transitioned to using the power chair and his own vehicle to get to and from work. His close friend continued to go with him for a couple months until the occupational therapist could finalize her assessment and approval for him to drive on his own. His friend moved the furniture around in his office to provide easy movement around the desk. A local agency, focused on ensuring individuals can return to work, set him up on voice-activated computer software and assisted with the vehicle modifications. Once again his office came to his aid, ensuring him a parking space that allows for his ramp and opening the door when he arrives. The building does not have self-opening doors. They also assist with those things such as placing food in the fridge, sweeping the office, carrying out the trash, watering plants, gathering items off the printer, etc.

My husband never would have been able to return without these friends and fellow associates. I was not strong enough to help him to and from work. It was exhausting for me just to help him get ready for work and to send him off with a healthy lunch. I never would have been able to transport him and spend that time in transit. These friends gave him the encouragement and physical support needed.

Work Considerations for All

I believe that returning to work is a healthy motivational option for many people—though that is clearly my opinion, not an opinion shared by all medical professionals. Therefore, what I have written is about our ongoing journeys to return to work. Working encourages us to get out and interact with the world as we did before. It is encouraging on the one hand and heartbreaking on the other as some people cannot see beyond our challenges. Those situations are difficult but not to be judged because I understand how hard it is to accept life that is different from our own.

I go into businesses and am impressed by those who struggle to get around each day and yet are working in many different roles. There are other people who are faced with visual challenges. There are still others who are working with challenges that cause pain or distress with no visible concerns.

Another thought is to encourage those who are challenged by a new twist in their lives to return either to work or to their social activities. And if neither is possible, to think about alternatives that they may enjoy. A woman and a man that I know through our church have always amazed me and were an inspiration during this time. They have found roles within the church. No one would fault them if they had chosen to only focus on their own challenges.

If someone used to work in an office but only has the energy now for an hour or two of work, do you know someone who could use a little assistance? Are they able to type papers or respond to correspondence? Are they able to do some piece work for a local seamstress or production facility? Are there community organizations that they could help with phone calls or mailings periodically? Do you have a newsletter that needs folded? Does a local church need baby blankets or sweaters knitted or crocheted? Endless possibilities!

It is also important to assist the caretaker in keeping their career on track if they so choose. If it is possible for the caretaker to pay someone while they go to work, don't hesitate to let them know if you have experience with a particular agency or individual. My neighbor gave me the names of several people she trusted. If you are able to stay with the patient on a scheduled basis, this is also a tremendous help. We never could have paid someone to care for me those seven months that I spent in bed. The loving support of family and friends who came and stayed with me so that my husband could go to work without worrying provided incredible peace of mind for both of us. Though we want to be there for our loved ones, we cannot be at our best 24/7 without re-energizing ourselves and working to maintain our own financial security.

Medical Concerns That Arise

My next book is going to be called, *Helping Others Through the Medical Maze*. This is not a book that describes care and treatment by any means. It will focus on the wonderful things people did for us related to our medical well-being and improvement. This section highlights a few examples. I will address most of these ideas within the next book.

I want to be clear—any medical considerations should

be verified with a certified medical professional. We were careful. I appreciated that my medical team was respectful of my questions and encouraged me to try non-traditional alternatives that they agreed were safe for my situation. I have found what is safe for one person may be harmful to another.

Such examples are the magnetics I used per the referral of a friend and the verification of my doctor before use. The magnetics were a tremendous help to me. I do know that one should not use magnetics if they have a broken bone that has not yet been properly set or if they have a situation where internal bleeding could be an issue.

Many people helped us with physical and occupational therapy. Again, it is important to verify what should be done. Encouraging the patient to do their physical and occupational therapy is so very important. Just trying to live can be exhausting at times so having someone else encourage exercise is awesome. Or someone willing to take a walk with you at less than 1 mile an hour. Or someone with unique knowledge, such as a friend who slowly and carefully encouraged me to do some chair yoga activities. And another friend who informed me about water physical therapy which then turned into being encouraged to attend a regular water class designed specifically for individuals who need gentle activities.

Whether a close family member, a distant family member, or a friend with interest or knowledge;

encouraging one to explore any activity to improve is critical to improvement. My cousin helped me over the fear of going from the walker to the cane. The physical therapist was working with me to do so though with the short amount of time we had together I was just too fearful to do any cane walking on my own. My cousin took the time to help me move beyond that fear. Again, being certain that it is approved by the professional.

Summary

∽ My Summary

This brings me to the life lesson of all life lessons. When a person is not at their best, they deserve a "boat load" of latitude; I don't mean a lifetime of latitude. A bad day or outburst should be taken in stride. An accidental honest comment such as, "This is a really bad time," or "Why didn't you call first," or "You know I should not eat this;" should be ignored and let pass. Such comments, whether delivered well or not well, are best treated as learning points, not offenses. Remember that the stressed or ill person is currently enduring many changes. We all know, after years of New Year's resolutions, that life changes are very challenging, especially when placed upon you. Therefore, a positive response to such a comment would be, "I am sorry, I did not realize." You could also then add to make sure the person does not feel bad about their comment, "What would be an example of a good treat to bring?" Note, though, that if you ask, then it would be best if you did some action to acknowledge your understanding. Either bring said item in the future or if part of a caring group, pass the knowledge forward.

That being said, unless there are mental complications involved, there is such a thing as patient responsibility. I know this may sound harsh to say because I am all about allowing people who are hurting latitude. My favorite saying to my consulting and coaching clients, "Assume positive intent until verified otherwise."

Therefore, it is my thought that first we assume positive intent on behalf of all parties and then we offer gentle boundaries as we go forward. I personally would much rather have someone set a gentle boundary with me instead of never returning to visit.

So, gifts given from the heart never deserve a broken heart. And a gift from the heart may be gently declined. This seems unclear without an example. Welcome feedback from anyone. If a person is trying to recover from a wound or serious injury, many medical professionals might suggest a high protein diet. If you choose a treat that is high in carbohydrates, then be accepting of gentle feedback that the patient won't be open to eating it. I suggest that you not take this as a break in your heart. And assume the person still recognizes your kindness.

We forget as patients and as friends that no matter the circumstance (barring mental trauma) all parties are responsible for any interaction. All of us have responsibility to try our best to act always with respect and consideration.

The patient must assume the responsibility to ask for help. A friend told me that people forget about you after six weeks. In my case, this definitely was not true. I believe people do not as much forget about you as much as perceive that they are no longer needed or even may be intruding. People say, "Call me if you need anything." They really do mean it. The injured or sick person must make the call no matter how hard it is to ask for help. I sometimes felt as if I might be bothering a person—especially the longer things continued. The giving/caring person could continue to suggest when they can and cannot be of help.

One of the first couples to see me in the hospital brought me a small pad and a pen. She said, "People want to help. Make a list of what you need." The notepad friend was right. Nobody is a mind-reader. I appreciate when family and friends continue to offer assistance in various areas especially with home chores, this book development, and paper organization. I believe that people appreciate when you encourage them to ask for help either from an individual, their church, or other organizations.

How is the caretaker holding up? Are they being brave and tough when they really need to know that many people are willing to help? Can the caretaker or spouse really take care of the injured spouse without hurting themselves? Do they need a mental or physical break? Would they feel guilty saying they need a break fearing that others would think they are not a caring individual? Always keep the dialog going and ask the tough questions. Pay attention to the current environment; don't tell the caretaker to take a needed break in front of the family member who needs the care.

Thank you for all you do for those you love. If you are reading this, I know there are people in your life who you care for with tenderness and generosity. Be gracious not only to others but also to yourself!

Journal

Journal of Key Events

I am determined to move forward in a positive direction! This book was written to mirror a positive world philosophy where people help each other through difficult times. I want a future filled with hope. I prefer to live my life in a way that consistently supports those around me. My goal is to make the world a better place when possible even if it is by me saying "please" and "thank you" to someone instead of using a sharp word. My husband laughs at me because I say "excuse me" and "thank you" to our dog. Please understand—there are days when it takes considerable energy and pure determination to move forward. And there are days I wish I could curl up in a ball and watch movies all day! Please don't judge yourself or others. Some days I must allow myself to be overwhelmed by life and ask for help along the way.

However, I have family members who depend on me so I must keep moving and complete life's required daily tasks. I am not able to curl up in that glorious little ball and watch TV all day. Especially since my injuries have slowed my pace dramatically. It takes all day many days to even tackle the most basic life sustaining activities and the required physical therapy. Honestly, some days I resemble a salmon attempting to swim upstream wondering if I will be able to reach my goal. Yet, the hope of reaching that goal is what keeps me on track.

My motivation also comes from the encouragement of

those around me. The inspiration to write this book was provided by a group of women I call my "inspiration team." They encouraged and motivated me to pursue this project. Life has frequently thrown distractions my way. The inspiration team gently nudged me to keep the momentum moving despite the daily struggles. Their belief in how this book will benefit others guides me. This keeps me grounded when I falter.

This book captures the caring supportive assistance gifted to my husband and me by family, friends, and strangers over the recent years. A side note: this book was started during the months I was bed-bound. I have continued to add stories to the book though I fondly remember other events that did not make it onto these pages. Through our ordeal, I have learned some of the hidden needs individuals face when life throws a curveball. I have experienced the healing impact generated when people come to our aid. People often appear "normal" and "composed" on the outside when their life is turned upside down. How do we watch for signs or inquire gently to truly know their struggles? There are some people, bless their hearts, who do pull off life with grace and composure no matter what adversity lands in their lap.

Too much happened at once for me to always remain composed. My goal in writing this book is to shine a light on the unbelievably kind gifts of time and resources that enabled us to continue forward. This guide helps us all remember how challenging even the most common task can become when our life is interrupted by a trauma or tragedy. My friends and family insisted I share more about the chain of events that inspired this book. I complied. Remember, though the pages that follow highlight portions of our journey, other people are facing critical junctures in their lives that are not as evident but are every bit as painful and disruptive. That is why, originally, I did not include our story within this book. I did not want the focus to be about us. My inspiration team insisted that the combination of the two provides the answers that you the reader may desire. Please assume that no matter what your pain, your friends and family want to understand how to offer you inspiration.

August 16, 2013
My Husband has Hip Replacement

We had been limited in the amount of hiking, biking, and walking we could do together because my husband had pain and limited mobility in his left hip. We were cautiously excited when he scheduled his hip replacement surgery for August of 2013—all surgeries are scary. My husband determined that the opportunity to once again be able to walk the dog daily, hike on the park trails year round, and travel without restriction outweighed any potential risk. Though it is considered a standard surgery these days, I took it very seriously to ensure the best healing environment and reduce the risk of infection. We did everything possible to be prepared. We even completed home tasks such as sanding and staining the porch floor the weekend before the surgery, moving a daybed into the living room, and acquiring entertainment options. I also packed a cleaning kit to sanitize his hospital room surfaces. We thought we were prepared.

Based on the pre-surgery class, our plan was that he would be partially weight bearing and, therefore, reasonably independent during his recovery. Instead, after the surgery, the doctor told us that for three weeks he was to be zero percent weight bearing. We were thrown off and concerned that something was wrong when we heard this news, especially since this translated into minimal physical or occupational therapy for the first three weeks. Clearly, he would need far more assistance than anticipated!

We needed to revamp our plan. How was he going to be able to get in and out of the house without placing weight on his new left hip? We needed new steps into the house. While at the hospital, I took the dimensions of the walker they provided. I raced home before the lumber yard closed, measured our current steps, designed the new steps, and ordered replacement wood cut to my specifications. Thank goodness for a prior relationship with the local lumber yard because in my frantic state, I forgot my purse and the lumber yard salesman allowed me to leave with the wood agreeing to pay him once they opened on Monday. My brother-in-law met me at our house and we put everything together just as if it were a kit—ok, he had to cut a few additional boards. These stairs prevented any accidental weight being placed on the hip as my husband used his walker.

Once home, we settled in with him using the recliner to reduce any pressure on the hip. I then slept on the daybed should he need assistance during the night. Thank goodness I did! His first trip to the bathroom resulted in absolute chaos. He tried to take the walker through the bathroom door only to discover that the bathroom had a very very narrow door. We lived in this house over 20 years—we never noticed. This resulted in a now emergency attempt to safely gain access to the bathroom and a horrible scene. If you ever have a planned procedure that requires the use of a walker or wheelchair, assess your home access throughout for safety issues and practice getting to the bathroom.

Concerned for his safety, I contacted the assigned home healthcare provider for guidance on how to keep him non-weight bearing while giving him access to the room of rest. Their answer, "We will be scheduling his appointment in a day or two." I very calmly explained that we needed guidance right away for a safe strategy.

Once again the woman stated, "The nurse must do her assessment first so it will be a day or two before we are able to provide physical therapy." After several minutes of trying to explain the risks involved, I broke down into hysterical tears—strangely, they then arrived within hours. I was surprised that tears trump rational behavior—go figure!!!

We were prepared with one strategy based on the education program we attended. We were very concerned when the healing parameters changed because all our planning had to be adjusted. As a result, his care consumed me. I placed clean sheets daily on every surface he used to reduce the risk of infection. Every surface he was exposed to was regularly sanitized. I spent an hour every morning cleaning the front porch so he could enjoy the company of friends who brought us dinner. I fed him only healthy food. When I needed unexpected supplies or prescriptions, I raced out to the store as quickly as possible. After the third week, he was released to partial weight-bearing status with continued motion restrictions. I stayed at home with him but now felt comfortable working on our landscaping that had been eliminated as the new front porch was built. I was also able to take him to a couple work meetings. At the end of the fourth week, he planned to drive to work on his own. It seemed as if I needed to get caught up on everything, having focused most of my attention on his care. We were clearly ready to get back to a normal existence and excited about the adventures upon which we were about to embark.

Saturday, September 14, 2013
Car Crashes Through the Post Office Entrance

I was so excited. I finally felt free to leave my husband home alone with the dogs. The plan was to run errands, work on the newly designed flower bed, and walk our dog and my brother-in-law's dog that we were watching for the weekend. It was a lovely day out and I was ready to no longer be trapped inside. I went to the post office to buy stamps. You may not want to read further if you are medically squeamish as I was prior to this crisis.

Chatting about the benefits of rubber mulch with my neighbor, my back to the post office entrance, I heard a horrible crash!!!! I turned to see the front grill of a car where the glass post office doors used to be, glass flying everywhere, and then it was over. I was pinned between the car and the inside post office lobby wall by a car that crashed through the two sets of entry doors and plowed into me faster than I could react.

I was unable to move. I screamed, "Get this thing off of me. This can't be happening! I need to be taking care of my husband!"

My neighbor took charge of getting the car backed away from me though it could not go far because it was stuck inside the post office lobby. I momentarily stood there on one leg leaning against the wall because my right leg was hanging contorted and sliced open. I opened up my arms and my neighbor lowered me to the ground where we worked together to hold my leg together. My left wrist was broken with my hand hanging at an odd angle—I don't even know how to explain the left wrist. I was awake the entire time thanks to my neighbor. I distinctly remember him using the words, "Stay with me." I recall thinking that is what they say on TV all the time—it must be important so I guess I better stay awake.

I was able to be calm because I thought the ambulance would be right there—our post office is located next to the emergency building. For some reason, no help came from next door—the ambulance took forever and actually came from across town. It is key to support the need for emergency care to be readily available. While they were working to place me on a back board, I heard someone question how they would get me out of the building since the car was blocking the doorway. I recall saying, "Someone needs to start breaking a window." Instead they were able to take me out over the hood of the car and through the back door.

On the way to the hospital, I asked to call my husband and one of the kind rescue team members gave me her cell phone. I wanted to talk to my husband because I was not sure if I would ever see him again. With the neck brace on, I was not able to hear his response. I was able though to tell him I loved him and to tell him to be careful not to hurt himself trying to see me at the hospital. I learned later that my neighbor who had helped me arrived at our house right around the same time I called. I asked my husband to contact my sister instead of my mother so that she could carefully share the news to others in the family.

They wheeled me into the operating room, a scene I had never previously experienced. I even avoided TV medical shows. Everything was so very bright and white. I heard snippets of conversation. Someone gently held my hand. "Can you feel me touching your toes?"

"Yes," I replied, adding the fearful question, "Will I lose my leg?"

"We are trying to keep that from happening."

I woke up in the recovery room. Everything seemed dark. I could not make out faces. I just heard the voices. A nurse, my husband, and my brother-in-law. My husband was very quiet. My brother-in-law was giving me a hard time about taking extreme measures to get attention. He explained later that the nurse gave him a nasty look to which he explained such that I could not hear, "If I don't give her a hard time, she will think she is dying—it's just the way we roll." I do recall when he suggested he leave and update the rest of his family waiting outside that I responded with a very clear request, "Don't even think about leaving right now because I need the distraction."

My brother-in-law commented once I was better how the nurse was amazing and took charge of my care. She was not sending me to a room until she was confident that the bleeding, which had once again started, was stopped.

I was in and out after that. I don't really remember the move from the recovery area to my intensive care room. I remember it being very dark and quiet. I remember asking the nurse where my husband was and she said he was not allowed in the room overnight and was out in the waiting area. I recall telling her that if he could not be in the room that they should have insisted he go home and get some rest. I did not realize they wanted him to be close by since they were not certain I would make it through the night. Thankfully, I had no idea for months as to how close to death I had come.

The nurse and I had one of those Abbott and Costello "Who's on first" conversations where people are not understanding each other. I was trying to ask her for a distraction. Anything to keep my mind occupied. Her response, "Honey, I am sorry but your blood pressure is too low so I am not able to give you pain medicine."

Strange how you clearly remember some things. I will never forget my response. "Honey, you don't understand. I just need a distraction. Please talk to me even if it is about what you are doing. Please turn on a radio or the TV. I can't take the quiet." She kindly turned on the TV and I felt much calmer.

I cannot imagine actually reading the volumes of medical records so I am explaining this part also from recollection and based on what others have since told me. I was told that my blood pressure was around 50/28 for about 8 hours. I was given 8 units of blood over the initial days. I spent roughly a month in intensive care. My leg was held together by a big metal contraption screwed directly into my bone with industrial looking screws. A leg version of Frankenstein. My leg was wrapped in what looked like kitchen plastic wrap with tubes flowing out of it into what is called a vac system—which is exactly that—a vacuum attached to your leg. It is like one of those travel bags where you suck out the air. In this case the two machines attached to my leg were sucking out all fluid entering the wound area. A major challenge is trying to keep the system sealed on a moving part of the body. When the seal would weaken, a horrible scary alarm would sound and only a limited number of hospital personnel were trained to handled the specialized bandaging system with an injury as complicated as mine. I had numerous surgeries over the months that followed. I still need additional surgical treatments yet to be scheduled.

My left wrist was badly broken and had to be surgically put back together though overall was largely ignored due to the complexities of the leg wounds. This, of course, delayed the recovery of my wrist.

Parades of medical professionals moved in and out of my room. Frequently several would stop by for the bandaging sessions asking, "Do you mind if I observe? Yours is a very interesting case." What a way to be defined! We will never be able to use the word "interesting" again per its normal definition. It seemed to us that in the hospital setting "interesting" meant this is a complicated, difficult case from which we all want to learn. I was thankful to have an incredibly focused and dedicated intensive-care staff.

October, 2013
Rehab Hospital Throws Me Out

On Friday morning, my last day in the hospital, into surgery I went in order to have what we called a fixator (or halo) bolted to my leg; literally, I mean you could build your house with these things! My leg looked like Frankenstein's head. My understanding was that the halo itself without the surgery cost approximately $10,000.

I was moved to a full-care rehabilitation hospital because my open wound still needed intensive care and bandaging. The fixator was intended to allow me full weight bearing use on that leg—tell that to the physical therapist who I now feel may have been fearful of my extensive leg bandaging and damage. Though understandable (it all looked very scary) this spurred the next devastating chain of events starting with physical therapy goals that did not take into account my true potential.

Therefore, when physical therapy did not measure my ability to place weight on the leg as was specified by the doctor, insurance gave me the boot while I was still dependent on others for all my care. The rehabilitation hospital case worker, entered my room on Monday morning, and said, "Insurance denied your claim on Friday. We are sending you home today after we send you out for some tests." Seriously, she knew on Friday before she left for the day and chose not to tell me until Monday morning when my husband was at work and I had no one to help me. I was terrified, hysterical, and panicked. I had spent the entire weekend in bed with nothing to do when I could have found help to prepare for my return home or had the opportunity to better determine my options for additional safe care.

If you have ever had anyone in the hospital, even for a planned surgery when you are at the top of your game, you know there are a ton of things that need to be done to prepare a home for a patient. From the basics of needing a bed, a means for the person to use the bathroom, and an opportunity to buy food and gather prescriptions. In this case, my husband and friends needed detailed training on how to care for my extensive injuries.

My wound was still wide open from my hip to just below my knee! The lower leg still needed daily fixator adjustments and medical care. I had very limited mobility using a walker with considerable difficulty and at tremendous risk of disturbing the vac system wrapping; thus, breaking the air tight seal. Plus, I had a hose running from my leg to a portable pump that traveled with me at all times. It was not possible for me to go upstairs to our bedroom or use our shower. Thank goodness we still had the daybed downstairs as a result of my husband's recent surgery.

I needed 24/7 care. I was not yet leaving my bed. I required extensive daily nursing care. I needed my fixator attachment bolts cleaned twice a day, I needed the fixator/halo bolt system adjusted twice daily, I needed my shrink wrap leg bandage changed every other day, I needed my vacuum system monitored and managed, I needed special authorization for strong pain medicine during the bandage changes, and I could not use my broken left hand. I believe that had the hospital appealed, insurance would have allowed me to stay at least an additional week, giving me the consistent wound care that I required—possibly even several more weeks. By not telling us the news on Friday, we were put in a position of panic and no opportunity to plan.

Several friends kept a close eye on me throughout my hospital journey. They kept me company when my husband was at work or needed to get things done at home. Two such friends happened to check in on me during the transition chaos and heard my panic. Upon further inquiry, they learned that I was not going to be able to afford the care I would need at home. Two friends volunteered to take on the incredible responsibility of caring for my leg every day until the end of the year. The cost of having a home healthcare nurse come twice a day was prohibitive. And my husband was not yet up to this after his hip replacement. These two friends dropped everything and raced to the rehabilitation hospital to learn how to make the precise fixator adjustments and to do the lower leg pin care that my leg required.

October, 2013
Transition to Home Health

Then, the transition to home healthcare did not go well. Most critical was the challenge that the first home healthcare nurse came to reapply my extensive shrink wrap system and did not know how to apply the vac system bandages properly. She removed the bandages and then could not figure out how to get new ones back onto my leg. I tried to help her as best I could. In the end, she just left leaving me lying there with my leg exposed to the environment and air! A second nurse arrived hours later. She was also unable to do the bandaging properly! She called in a vac system specialist who left her home in a horrible rain storm to arrive at 9:30 that evening to provide instruction.

I ended up with a serious infection and an additional surgery which delayed the healing process and required skin grafts.

For the duration of the vac system application, the specialist came to every bandaging appointment providing instruction for the team of two nurses and reassurance to me along the way. The specialist gave me her number to call 24/7 if there were any concerns. She communicated via text with the plastic surgeon to determine when the wound had healed enough for the next procedure to be performed.

October 2013 to May 2014
A Winter in a Cocoon

Daily nurse visits for critical medical care, daily friend visits to care for what they called pin care, and daily scheduled friends to stay with me to provide safety and sustenance support. Initially it required two nurses and the instruction of a vac system specialist to change my bandages. The home nursing care continued well into the following year.

The way home-care insurance works, anyone from the home-care agency counts as a visit and visits are often severely limited depending on insurance plans. We sacrificed all physical and occupational therapy due to the extreme medical bills that were piling up. Looking back, this was definitely not the best way to go—we were wrong. How is a person struggling to recover able to know the options and the strategies that make the most sense?

Until the skin graft surgery in November, I was encouraged to limit my movement because any tiny opening in the bandages resulted in an alarm indicating a leak. The specialist was always comforting and reassuring; she would walk me through options and come first thing the next morning.

After the skin graft surgery in November, the medical appointments were reduced gradually to every other day and then to every three days, etc. At this point, when there were many medical professionals involved, the recommendations were confusing. Move around. Ignore the nerve pain. Stay off your leg. Place full weight on leg. Elevate to reduce swelling.

I was very weak. I lacked sleep and the future was scary. It was very difficult to make decisions regarding potential treatments. I went in for two more in-hospital surgeries, one being the extensive skin grafting of my right leg. I also negotiated to have three surgeries that were normally performed under anesthesia to be completed outpatient in the doctor's office.

My lower leg kept increasing in size due to the damage to my lymph system—my foot felt like I was trying to walk on a balloon. I was not able to fit my foot into any type of shoe which limited my ability to walk outside or for any distance inside. After repeated inquiries to the surgeon, he said, "You are not going to like the look of your leg. You will just have to live with it."

A friend told me about lymphedema treatments. It took some research, but I found a resource that could help me through compression wrapping. These treatments resulted in increasing my mobility. I could now wear a man's large tennis shoe on my right foot and begin to walk and drive once again. In addition, the high infection risk lymph fluid was greatly reduced through the use of compression.

Throughout this entire process, the healing aspect and expense consumed our energy, so I was not receiving therapy on my leg or my hand. Once therapy started, I did my assigned exercises daily and became very concerned that I would never regain any range of motion in my wrist. I was unable to lift even the lightest item without pain. I expressed my concern to the doctor. He replied, "Use your hand!" Why was he the first person to share this great advice? I learned that one should never give up. Today, my left wrist, though it often hurts and is clearly not very strong, can in fact type and bend as it did before.

With my leg I spent hours of walking in circles using the walker inside my house. My ability to stand or walk on my own was not improving. I was so unsteady that I feared leaving the support and protection afforded by the walkers. My cousin told me that if I did not use the cane, I would never be able to use the cane. With that new knowledge, I started making progress on walking.

As you can imagine, the paperwork from a medical issue of this nature was overwhelming. Each entity and individual within that entity seems to send multiple bills. It was stressful not knowing how many bills were going to come and if we would be able to pay them. We sacrificed care because of cost and often times just not knowing what care was available. I was not sure what the best way is to find out possible patient options. I often felt as if the medical professionals spent energy determining what insurance would cover rather than outlining available options.

October 2013 to May 2014
Without Friendships Recovery Is Unbearable

The outstanding care of many medical professionals kept me alive and made it possible for me to walk again.

The outstanding outreach of family, friends, and strangers is what gave me the strength and the initiative to keep up the fight and move forward in my life. Their encouragement and guidance is what inspired this book and future books. Without them, I know it would have taken great strength and commitment not to curl up in a ball and give up.

If we had needed to hire a home nurse to stay with me, we would definitely have been financially ruined. Instead, friends and strangers who became friends came and stayed with me. Many would bring lunch and chat. Others would bring projects to complete or organize all of the medical supply boxes stacked everywhere. Several would shop for needed items and set them up within the house.

My sister came for a week after my skin graft surgery. She did all kinds of projects around the house including cob web removal and a good solid sweeping. She and my childhood friend completed a wall art project that I had started right before being hit—it took them almost an entire day. They did a lovely job and it turned a pile of clutter into something lovely to look at. My sister sewed items for me to make my life more beautiful and easier. She gave my husband a week off from every day activities since I was only allowed out of bed to use the bathroom.

Other friends helped me with my recovery therapy by either teaching me chair/bed yoga or walking in circles within the house with me. Once the weather warmed up, they went for walks down the sidewalk with me—very slow walks!

Family members changed traditional holiday plans to encourage our participation. They went out of their way to set up the logistics to get me in and out. They even moved their furniture to support my injuries.

Other friends offered input regarding questions to ask our medical professionals such as could I use a bone stimulator, would magnetics be safe, what supplements would help with the healing, and what therapy options were available? They also offered to share their experiences and knowledge regarding insurance policies.

Once I was able, friends offered transportation and outings to allow us to escape the confines of our home.

Family members took our furry child, our dog, into their home, bringing her to visit and sending photographs of her enjoying her stay.

I was able to move forward thanks to the compassion and care shared with me over the last few years.

May 12, 2014
A Tornado—Nope—Ground Saturation

After an entire winter in bed, spring brought hope of getting outside. Or at least that was what I thought.

"Honey, could we please watch something other than the storm tracking? We have already had our disaster for the year. We are not going to get hit by a tornado." Those were the words I uttered literally 10 minutes before we heard a life changing rumble. On May 12, 2014, while I was still spending most of each day in bed, our house started making horrible cracking sounds. We thought we were hearing the freight train rumble of a tornado hitting our house. My husband ran to the front door while I hobbled to the interior bathroom. When he saw that all was calm outside, my husband rushed to the basement door thinking I had tried to get downstairs. He started screaming my name panicked that I was under several feet of mud that was now in our basement. After I assured him I was in the

bathroom, he exclaimed that we no longer had a back basement wall.

When the emergency crews arrived, it was confirmed that 30 feet of our 35 foot wall had collapsed creating a seven foot mud slide sink hole in our back yard that was now in our basement. Ground saturation. Unbeknownst to us, the wall took out the hot water tank which then proceeded to fill the basement to ground level floating our belongings out into our backyard as our basement overflowed. One never realizes how many key components exist in one's basement.

All of the emergency contractors who advertise that they know what to do when you have a home disaster had waiting lists of people with water in their basements—there was considerable flooding in the area. One of the company owners when I called said, "Insurance probably won't cover this so you better just get down there and start digging out." I could not believe his rudeness! Even if I was not injured, we are talking about a very dangerous situation for someone who is not trained. Our house was literally suspended on weakened corners with no wall in between. The entire house would have caved in without the quick reactions of friends and family.

We needed someone to drain the basement, empty the contents including cement block and mud, replace the wall, and keep the rest of the house from being consumed by the hole. In addition, everything had to be replaced: furnace, sump pump, air conditioner, electrical panel, security system, phone connection, back-up sump pump, electrical outlets, stairs, built-in shelving units, and built-in cabinets. Of course all the contents were ruined. We filled two over-sized dumpsters (hard to obtain due to the local storm damage). Unfortunately, since I was still only able to wear things like scrubs, I was storing most of our clothing, shoes, and many household items in the basement—thus I was left with a very limited wardrobe.

My husband and our dog stayed at our friends' house while I slept in the car at our house waiting for the electricity to be turned off—before that night I had only driven the short distance from physical therapy and home so it was scary. At 5am I went to our porch contractor's house and sat in his driveway until he left for work at 6am. I told him what happened. He immediately headed to the equipment rental store and rented a heavy duty pump to drain the basement while he went to work. He got the last pump available to be rented. Once drained, with the help of our nephew, they built a makeshift support wall. Friends and the contractor's team then spent an entire Saturday cleaning out the basement, mostly into a dumpster. Friends worked hard to salvage a few items by putting them into the garage or on the lawn for future examination. Once again, the emergency recovery companies were of no assistance. I recently saw a commercial that said they work to preserve your memories. I really could have used their help saving mine!

The contractor, a mason, handled the actual wall reconstruction over the course of a month. I found and contracted with electricians, a plumber, the security company, and the heating and cooling professionals. This task was harder than normal because the area storms had impacted so many households and companies were busy.

Friends and family cleared out the food from the refrigerator and freezer since there was no power to the home and all would go bad if left inside. And since I was not able to lift and carry items, they helped us transfer critical belongings to the house of our friend with whom we stayed. Staying in our friend's first floor bedroom just down the street from our house was extremely helpful since, with my ongoing leg care needs and high risk for infection, I was not comfortable staying in a more public environment.

There is still basement work to be finalized, the yard to be reclaimed, a deck to be rebuilt, the main floor drywall to be repaired, a few windows to be replaced, and the sliding door to be replaced. Plus a ton of paperwork yet to be completed. As this book goes to press, these tasks still remain in progress as we continue efforts to recover.

The day we were able to move back into our house, (because the structure was sound and the utilities restored—not because the house was in any way finished), my husband had a stroke!

June 9 , 2014
The Caretaker Becomes the Patient

The house is not yet finished. There are still cracks in the walls and doors that do not open. We loved staying with our kind friends. They are amazing people. As they say, there is nothing like the comfort of home and we thought that we had imposed long enough even though they never ever gave us any indication that we were anything but welcome.

I was still using a cane at the time and only driving

within the neighborhood. Thankfully friends once again came to my aid. They met me at the house to clean and carry in our belongings. I was still unable to climb stairs so their help was invaluable.

Our friends left, and I was ready to elevate my leg and relax. I knew my husband would handle dinner as soon as he came home from work.

Instead, our dog barked, letting me know my husband was home. She continued to bark when he did not come to the door. I could not figure out what was taking him so long. I went to let our dog out to greet him and instead found him covered in mulch at the base of our porch steps lying in the flower garden. I called my neighbors and they came over to help.

My husband had a stroke. We were blessed that it did not impact his cognitive function. He spent approximately six weeks in a rehabilitation hospital, six weeks in a skilled nursing facility, and then about a month at a small brain injury intensive therapy facility that a friend found for him. I would never have been able to bring him home with my injuries without the extensive physical and occupational therapy which gave him the strength to transfer with assistance from his wheelchair to bed.

We aggressively scheduled the recommended therapy. The wonderful trained professionals guided us each step of the way with new exercises and occupational therapy. My husband worked for hours each day just to be able to move a finger or his right leg. A healthcare aide came three times a week to help him get cleaned up and to teach him how to once again dress himself. We bought men's pajama pants without buttons and larger T-shirts to make it easier for him to dress. He worked hard with the encouragement of so many as friends and professionals who provided therapy and care throughout the day.

Through friends we found the brain injury rehabilitation facility, government agencies that help return brain injury patients to work, medical resources that helped me regain the ability to walk, and the list continues. Since I was not able to care for my husband on my own, friends, family, and neighbors would assist me in getting him from the house to the car and from the car to appointments. Friends would pick us up for special events or provide a dinner on their driveways since we could not get him into their houses.

Friends encouraged my husband to gradually return to work. His officemates bought and set up a laptop computer for him to work from home for an hour a day at first, then built up his time a bit each week. Gradually, friends started driving him into the office for a few hours and then built up his time on site also. The balance was a challenge because the physical and occupational therapy times were also critical as was the clear need for resting time. And as anyone who has ever experienced a medical concern knows, the number of doctor appointments and tests is an ongoing battle to address.

March 1, 2017
The Story Continues

When my first draft of this book was passed around for review by my inspiration team, there were only five sentences describing what had happened to us. The feedback was that I needed to share more details about our journey.

The review of the second draft came back with the comment—how are you doing today? So here is a brief status at the point this book was published.

With my husband now unable to assist with home projects it has been financially impossible to address any of the projects we were in the middle of completing—they continue to be undone. Prior to my being hit, the two of us had worked under the guidance of skilled carpenters to focus on many home remodeling initiatives. We had just managed and helped to build our new front porch. At the time everything started to happen, the porch still needed to be completed and the siding needed to be replaced. We had put in a new large front garden which was meant to be our summer project. Of course now being financially constrained, we have not been able to complete any of these projects or finalize the basement repairs.

A key part of this is the financial strain of medical expenses. Neither of us has been able to work at our prior capacity. Tasks that we used to be able to complete on our own now have to be completed by those we pay. An example is that the basement and main floor walls require being painted and we cannot do that type of work on our own as we did in the past. My husband used to share in the cooking, cleaning, lawn mowing, gardening, winter shoveling, painting, and remodeling. We are not able to afford to pay for all these services. We are grateful to our friends as they continue to support us in so many ways. Friends have weeded, cleaned, mowed, and cooked. We would enjoy caring for others in the future as we were able to do in the past.

Our inability to get around has also had an emotional and physical impact on our parents. My husband was unable to spend time with his mother during her final years. I have been unable to go assist my mom as I did in the past because I an unable to leave my husband for more than a brief duration and it is impossible for him to go to her house because there is no handicap access. I feel I am missing critical family time with my mother.

My husband and I are positive people by nature. And on those days when it is difficult to be positive, we encourage each other to keep moving forward in a positive way. I am encouraging him with his work and ongoing extensive therapy requirements. He is encouraging me to complete this book and return to the work that I love. It is difficult though because normal daily tasks require extra time and effort.

This past Thursday is a key example. My husband had a work appointment at 8am. A rehabilitation doctor appointment at 11am. An eye specialist appointment at 3:10pm. And physical therapy at 6:30pm. In between those appointments we needed to ensure he had proper nutrition and some time to rest. The day was exhausting.

It is frustrating that it takes me forever to complete tasks such as laundry and grocery shopping due to my injuries. Since I am still only able to carry small loads of clothing or groceries, it means several trips. My movements are slow based on my injuries and my need to hold the stairway railing very firmly to help pull me up the steps. This means that clutter and paperwork build up as we work to live on the first floor of a two story house. It is all very frustrating, overwhelming, and at times discouraging.

Life is still difficult. Each day has challenges and blessings.

So though there are days when I wake up and struggle to believe that this all keeps happening, there is always the knowledge that others, whether family, friends, or strangers, need your help. And though some days you really want to curl up in a ball and never move, hope of a better tomorrow prevails!

The support of family, friends, and complete strangers has brought us to where we are today and has given us strength and courage to face what the future will bring. This journey and the encouragement of so many is what inspired this book. Joy can be found. Hope does prevail thanks to the knowledge and kindness provided by those who are in our lives. And I myself, though I always tried to be there for others, never had any idea of how much it really impacts one's life. Because this is to me the most important phrase within the book, I am choosing to repeat it here. Whatever you choose to do for another, if it is done from the heart, don't hesitate! And whether you are the patient or the caretaker, there is always an opportunity for kind-hearted communication.

Made in the USA
Monee, IL
04 November 2026

67387515R00105